finding
Angela Shelton

finding
Angela Shelton

THE TRUE STORY OF
ONE WOMAN'S TRIUMPH
OVER SEXUAL ABUSE

BY ANGELA SHELTON

Meredith Books
1716 Locust Street
Des Moines, Iowa 50309–3023
meredithbooks.com

Cover illustration by Matt Mahurin

Library of Congress Control Number: 2007938175

ISBN: 978-0-696-23941-0

Printed in the United States of America.

For Anonymous.
Thank you for taking the leap. I will never forget you and
the impact you have had on my life.

*This book is dedicated to all survivors of sexual abuse, domestic violence,
and neglect. Thank you for your encouragement, love, support, and resiliency.
Please spread the word so that more of us will find help, healing,
and wholeness. I love you.*

Part I

Searching for Angela Shelton

Day 1 of the search
Los Angeles, 2001

I have a big mouth. If I had kept it shut I wouldn't be staring at a 33-foot motor home right now. I'm about to drive it around the country and meet other women who share my name.

I'm a writer in Hollywood and I was faced with the writers' strike. I had to figure out what to do during that time. Most of the people I know in the business were working on reality TV shows. Some were working on documentaries. The only thing that came to my mind quickly was to write a theater piece about my life. I had already written a movie called *Tumbleweeds* about my mother and I was brainstorming other experiences in my life to write about while I was meeting with HBO. I was there pitching another movie and the producer asked me if I had any ideas for a documentary. I laughed and offhandedly suggested that I drive around the country and meet every other Angela Shelton and call it *Searching for Angela Shelton*.

I'm not really Angela Shelton. I changed my last name when I was 18, and I've always loved my chosen name. Angela Shelton has a ring to it that I like a lot.

"I could go meet myself through all the women in America," I suggested. "I've looked myself up before. There are many of us. I was trying to put together a theater piece around my name too. But a documentary would be awesome."

"I love it!" the producer said.

"It could be really inspirational to women actually, uniting them through one name."

"I think it's awesome," she said. "And it's really funny. You can collect all the Angelas and go to Vegas. We could have an Angela Shelton convention with matching hats and jackets. You could even have a big bus with *Searching for Angela Shelton* along the side. Hysterical." She clapped her hands together and reached for her phone. We had a hit.

I was walking on cloud nine when I got home. HBO was going to fund my idea! I was so sure of it that I pulled up AOL People Finder and found various Angela Sheltons all over the country and started calling them. The first Angela I called was in the shower.

"What are you saying? You're doing what? Let me dry off for a second." As she toweled herself off, I told her my idea to survey women and use the name Angela Shelton as the vehicle to meet them. "I'd be really interested in that. I'd like to see who all the other Angelas are. I like this idea," she said, both assuring me and pushing me forward. So I started questioning her as she was dripping wet. She told me she was married and had twin boys. She worked in the medical field. Her mother died when she was 5 years old and her father raised her. "I've had to deal with a lot of death," she said. "But I had a really good father. He was very protective of me. I'm lucky to have him." I couldn't believe how open she was about her life. I started to tell her about my dad, but I felt bad that I caught her in the shower.

"I better let you get dressed. I'll let you know how the movie is coming and when I'll be arriving in your town."

"That's just great. I have to go tell everyone that I'm going to be in a movie."

I hung up and stared at the phone, thinking about random women telling me about their lives. I quickly called another one and another one and they all started sharing.

"This is funny! I love this idea."

"I wasn't born a Shelton. I married one."

"That's OK; this isn't about the name. This is about women," I said.

"Are you sure you're not a telemarketer?"

"Girl, you want to hear about my life? I could write a book."

"Do you have a few hours?"

"What haven't I been through is the real question."

"A survey? Well, I'm divorced and very happy about it. I threw a party."

"Me too," I said.

"Is that really you in that movie about your mom?"

"No, I wasn't in it. I wrote it. Cowrote it actually with my ex-husband. I better say that so he doesn't fly off the handle. It's based on me and my mom."

"And now you're making a documentary? That's so neat. I know all about men flying into rages, let me tell you. Are you sure you're not a telemarketer?" I laughed out loud like I did when any of them asked me that. I looked up at the clock and realized I'd been on the phone for hours. I looked at my collection of notes on all of them and realized I was hooked on Angela Sheltons.

"I love your voice," the Angela in Virginia said.

"You do? I've always hated my voice."

"No, it's great. There's something about it that makes me just want to talk to you. I can't wait to meet you."

"How are we all doing so far?" the Angela Shelton in Detroit asked me.

"Amazing. Most of you are nurses."

"Me too," she said.

"There's an alcoholic Angela too who keeps calling me almost every night ever since I left the first message about this movie."

"Bless her. I will pray for her. When are you going to get here? My husband thinks this is a big joke. Can't you come now?"

"I have to wait for funding first, but I'll hopefully see you in about a month."

"You just hit the road and trust that it will work out. There's always going to be bills. You just know that this is going to be a blessing for all of us. I'm praying for you. I know I was meant to answer the phone that day you called. I think this movie is blessed. You wait and see. When are you getting here? My husband is just staring at me, shaking his head. He doesn't believe you're coming."

"I'll be there. I'm leaving on May 2 because the strike is supposed to begin on the first."

But the strike didn't happen and HBO passed on my idea. The producer called me to apologize and said that she hoped that I hadn't spent too much time working on the project.

"The higher-ups loved your idea, but we're already funding another documentary where a guy is doing the same thing," she said.

"Surveying women?"

"No, he's inviting all of his namesakes over for dinner. There are 12 of them."

"Twelve men with the same name having dinner?" I tried to explain that my idea had nothing to do with my name and was more of a way to meet random women than to make a movie about my name. But HBO passed.

"I know, but the higher-ups have spoken and we can't fund you. But I love your idea. Maybe you should just go do it on your own," she suggested. Crap. I hung up and stared at my stack of Angela Shelton notes. I thought about the one running to tell all her friends that she was going to be in a movie. I didn't want to call them all up again and tell them a big fat never mind. I wanted to meet them. I had come to think that my offhand idea was actually a really good one. I wanted to make this movie for the Angelas as well as to prove that I could do it without the help of a big studio.

So I threw a party. I sent out invites to all 300 people in my address book to raise the money. Some were people I had known all my life, some I met a few times, and some I don't recall ever meeting. I wrote a treatment about how I planned to drive around the country and survey women in America who all happened to be named Angela Shelton. I told them how most of the Angelas were nurses and ranged from age 22 to 48, and they all had a story to tell. I explained how the Angelas covered a wide variety of women from one who lived on a golf course and didn't work to one who managed a Taco Bell. I asked people to invest or donate, and I enclosed a self-addressed stamped envelope in the party invite just for the hell of it. People actually sent me checks. That's how I got the money to rent the RV that I'm staring at now. I hope I don't disappoint all of them.

I asked a few filmmaker friends of mine how to get a crew together and, more important, how to make a movie. I've never directed before; I've only written. The best advice I received was to not think about it and just do it, so that's what I'm doing. I was told that the best thing to do is set a date and stick to it and everything will fall into place. "Making a movie is like having a baby; you're never ready for it. The date comes and the train leaves the station."

My train looks like a Bounder motor home. I have taken the leap and announced that I'm officially making this movie. My four crewmembers have agreed to go on the road with me even though I'm not funded like I thought. I haven't told them that I only have $1,500 left in my account. I have no idea how I'll keep them paid or fed, and I have to pick them all up at sunrise.

I pour myself a glass from the last champagne bottle and wonder if I can pull this off. Maybe I've lost my mind. The launch party for the documentary is over, and I'm alone in the house staring out the window. The RV has a halo of light around it from the full moon. I leave in five hours. I'm not sure I've planned this trip very well. My shoulders are so tense they ache. Maybe I should have waited for another production deal, but I couldn't cancel the trip just because I didn't have the money. Angela Sheltons are expecting me. I have to believe that this will all work out somehow. I close the map of the U.S. that I have covered in stars to represent each town that holds an Angela. I slide the red binder that is filled with all the Angela Sheltons' contact information into my backpack. I'm actually doing this. There are 32 women so far. I only have one or two days scheduled with each of them. I hope it's enough time to dive into their lives and gauge how women are doing. Then I'll come back to Los Angeles, find an editor, get the film into Sundance, and prove that I can make a film so I can direct my comedy. I have it all planned.

The phone rings as I take another swig of lukewarm champagne. I answer it without looking at the caller ID, thinking it must be another friend wishing me farewell.

"Why the hell are you calling me?" It's the alcoholic Angela Shelton. I recognize her voice immediately. I've spoken to her more than any other Angela.

"What do you mean, why am I calling you? You called me." She doesn't answer, just laughs and gulps back a swig of beer.

"I'm leaving tomorrow."

"For where?"

"To go on this trip." I realize she must be really drunk. I've only told her about this movie more than 10 times. She keeps telling me she doesn't want to be involved, but I figure if I keep her on the phone long enough she might agree to let me come meet her. Then I can put a star sticker on her town on my Angela Shelton map. "I told you 100 times already, I'm going to meet all the Angela Sheltons in America. *Searching for Angela Shelton.* Remember?" She laughs like we're old friends and I'm sharing another one of my harebrained ideas.

"And they all spoke to you?"

"A lot of them thought I was a telemarketer or an identity thief when I first called. But after I explained that my name is Angela Shelton also and I'm doing a survey of women, they opened up and talked to me. But none of them call me like you do. You take the cake as far as time goes."

"This is so stupid. Who would want to watch this? I mean, why Angie Shelton?"

"Because it's my name. It could be Barbara Smith for all I care. It's because it's my name and I like my name."

"See, I can't be in this movie."

"Why, is Shelton your married name?"

"Yes," she says like she has a get-out-of-jail-free card.

"That doesn't matter. There are quite a few Angelas who have Shelton as their married name. It's not about the name; this is about us as women. I could have picked any name. I just happen to like mine. And I think the Angela Sheltons represent all women in a way. I think you represent women too."

"Even though I'm drunk off my ass?"

"Yes," I say as I pour out more lukewarm bubbly.

"But there must be like 500,000 Angie Sheltons."

"I found 76 of them on the Internet. Most of them were disconnected. Well, 21 were. I left messages for about 55 Angelas. Not all of them called me back though."

"You're freaking me out."

"'Cause you're going to be in a movie? Who cares? I'll just show up and talk to you. I can block out your face if you want. And it's just a name. You know, I'm not even Angela Shelton."

"What? You are freaking me out. This is weird."

"I chose that name when I was 18."

"Why?"

"Because I didn't want my dad's name," I answer. She pauses for a good long time. I hear her light a cigarette.

"Is this going to be on TV?"

"Maybe. I hope it will be in movie theaters. That's my plan."

"Why are you doing this? It's so stupid."

"I told you already. I'm a screenwriter. I cowrote that movie *Tumbleweeds*, remember? I was up for writing another movie for HBO, and the producer asked me if I had any new ideas for a documentary."

"This is going to be on HBO?"

"No, HBO passed on it. It's perfect though actually. It's better to be independent. I have more freedom that way. So I'm making the film through my production company." I sound so official. Little does she know that my company is just a name. "But when HBO passed, I had already started calling all of you, and the similarities of our lives are amazing. They've all grown on me, these Angelas, especially you."

"You don't know me. You can't come see me."

"Then why do you keep calling me all the time?" She is silent. "All of the other Angelas are really excited about this."

"I bet."

"And you want to know what's sad?"

"What?"

"They all told me about their lives. And most of them have been raped, beaten, or molested at least once, some of them more than once. Some survey, huh?" I tap a cigarette out of the pack while that fact sinks in. Angela pauses and sort of laughs and hiccups at the same time. I wait.

"Well, that makes me feel much better."

"Yeah, right. Me too." I light my cigarette. We both inhale and exhale smoke.

"They just came out and told you that?"

"After we were on the phone for a while. They asked about my past and why I wanted to survey women in America. I told them that I wanted to see how women were doing. I told them about my past and how I was abused. I needed to tell them something about myself so they didn't hang up on me. I had to prove I wasn't a telemarketer." Angela laughs loudly. "But it has certainly shown me that once you share something about yourself, you give someone else the freedom to share. After I told them about me, that's when I found out more about them." She doesn't respond. I wonder if I just pushed her away or pulled her to me. "I've spoken to each Angela for at least an hour so far, sometimes much longer. But you take the cake as far as time goes. I've talked to you more than any other Angela."

"Really?" She seems touched but then gets defensive. "You never told me about your life."

"Yes, I did."

"When?"

"You were drunk. You probably don't remember." I exhale. Angela does the same.

"Yeah, probably."

"How much do you drink anyway?"

"About a case of beer a night."

"Angela! It's a wonder that hasn't killed you."

"Yeah, too bad, right?" I hear her take another swig. "Why are you doing this?"

"Oh God, Angela. How many times are you going to ask me that? I'm doing it to survey women. We just all happen to be named Angela Shelton, and we all have a story. And I need to finish packing. I'm leaving in the morning." I look up at the clock and see that it's the next morning already. Crap. "I guess in a lot of ways I'm searching for myself too through all these women," I admit. "That's what my therapist says anyway. But I don't really want to be in the movie."

"Me either." We both laugh.

"Maybe the Angelas will all be so amazing that both of us can hide from the camera."

"Yeah, I'm invisible." I don't know what to say to that. I just listen to her smoke. "So don't come by here. Don't come see me. I can't be in this movie."

"How come?"

"Because I'm nobody."

"Oh jeez, Angela. Yes, you are somebody. You're Angela Shelton." Silence. I hear a train go by on her end. It sounds like it runs right through her living room. "I love that sound." We silently listen to it roar past her house.

"The train has left the station. I'll never be on that train." Angela takes a swig of beer. "And your father?" she asks, just like that, out of the blue. It stuns me for a second. I cough.

"My father?" I try to recall if I've told her the full story or not. I can only hear the sound of her exhaling cigarette smoke. "Why do you ask about my father?"

"Oh, my father . . ." Angela trails off into a drunken mumble. "I can't talk about my father." She starts mumbling about her father, and I wonder whose story I'm listening to, mine or hers.

January 2001—four months before the search
Preproduction, Los Angeles

My therapist thinks that *Searching for Angela Shelton* is going to be cathartic for me, but I haven't felt any real catharsis yet. To be completely honest, I didn't even know what that word meant. I had to look it up. It means a purging and purification through art, which fits, I guess, because I'm making a movie. I'm an artist. Maybe I'll be purified. Maybe I'll purge. "Catharsis" also means a spiritual renewal.

"I think that your intuition is further ahead than you are," my therapist says. "By setting out on this journey, it's like your subconscious is the bow of the ship, far ahead of you, knowing your journey before you do. It is like your subconscious is seeing through the storm so to speak. Don't you think it's meaningful that you're calling it 'Searching for Angela Shelton'?" She's hinting at the fact that I'm searching for myself. I don't bite at her bait.

"It's so messed up that most of them have been abused, raped, molested, victims of domestic violence, you name it. I didn't even filter them or pick only the ones with pasts like that; I just called them all up randomly. And most of them have horror stories. That really does say something about women in general, doesn't it? Hopefully this film can help women become stronger and get out of abusive situations. Maybe it will show our society that we have a big problem. And I thought it was going to be funny."

"But we're here to talk about how it affects you, not the other Angela Sheltons," my therapist points out. "Does what happened to you make you angry? You've talked a lot about how what happened to the other Angelas makes you angry, and you've also said how angry you get about what happened to your stepsister, but I've never heard you talk about being angry at what happened to you." I hate therapy.

I don't answer. It is so much easier to be angry and compassionate about what happened to the other Angelas and to my stepsister. But I don't know how to be angry for myself. It's like that part of me is numb, asleep, silent. It's as though if I start to feel anger, it will overtake me and I'll become like a Tasmanian devil, twirling around, spitting fire and rage. So I don't respond. I look at the clock and see that, luckily, my session is over.

1975

I went to live with my dad when I was 3 years old. He left my mom for her best friend who had two kids. My new stepmother left her husband just as suddenly. My dad and my mom had been friends with my new stepmother and her former husband for a long time. They spent a lot of time together.

They traveled, shared hotel rooms, went bowling together. Then the day came when my dad and my soon-to-be stepmother visited my mom. They came to the trailer we lived in and told my mom that they were running off together to get married. Their decision required that she sign the divorce papers. My mom didn't fight it. She signed. She seemed kind of happy to get rid of my dad. She didn't even cry. She had never even really liked my dad. She had only married him to get away from her abusive mother. And she didn't have any hard feelings toward her ex-best friend, even though my soon-to-be stepmother refused to look her in the eye. The only thing that upset my mother was that my dad wanted custody of me, and I was the only thing that my mom wanted.

That's when my dad hired a lawyer for himself. He had more money than my mother. He insisted that it was better for me to live with him and his new instant family. He could provide for me.

My mother had spent the nine years of married life with my dad working to put him through school. She was a bank teller with no degree, and my dad fought her for me. They had never fought over anything before, nor had they had an argument. They didn't even talk much. They spent most of their time watching TV together. The only time my mom put her foot down about anything was when I was born. She told my dad flat out that she wasn't going to work one day until I had reached the age of 3. She told him that he'd better get a job to support her and me, so he did. And when I turned 3, my dad left my mom for another woman who had two young children.

My mom's family said that I should live with my dad too. They didn't believe that a single mother should have a child when the child had the option of a complete family, especially since my now-single mother didn't go to church. My dad went to church all the time, which made him a better parent in my Grandmother's eyes.

My mom wanted the best for me. She wanted to be a better mother than her own mom and she didn't want to hold me back like her mom had done to her. My grandmother had never let my mom make decisions, so my mom asked me whom I wanted to live with. I was 3 years old, and my only thought as I looked out the window at the road I'd be going down was that my new stepmother made Kool-Aid. My mother was beginning to think sugar was a drug and wouldn't have something like Kool-Aid in the house. I wanted cherry-flavored Kool-Aid, so I told my mom that I wanted to live with my dad. I wanted a brother and sister, and a cat, and a dog, and Kool-Aid. My mom was sad. She wondered if it was a good idea to ask a 3-year-old where she wanted to live, but when my mom's entire family and the lawyers told her that she should let me go to my dad's, she let me go.

Once I was there, my dad's lawyer told my mom's lawyer that for my own safety my dad should have full custody of me. He said it was because of my asthma. My asthma was getting worse, and my dad and his lawyer said they were worried about what would happen if I had to go to the hospital and they couldn't get in touch with my mom to get permission to help me. It was better for my health if my dad had full custody of me. Mom tried to fight with them, but she was concerned for my health too. Her lawyer told her not to worry about anything. She was assured that she would still have visitation even though my dad had full custody. My dad promised my mom that she could visit me whenever she wanted and Mom believed him. She signed over full custody.

Dream Journal—May 2, 2001

I dreamed about a dark house. There was a dead body in a body bag that I was trying to pull down a dark hallway as quickly as I could. It was leaking foul liquid. I tried not to get the liquid on my feet as I pulled the body bag toward the light in the doorway. I was being followed. I could hear the footsteps approaching me. All I knew was that I had to get the body out into the light.

I woke up feeling scared and disgusted. I can still smell that rancid smell. I feel like I should go back to sleep and deliver the body through the door. I wonder what that means. Maybe it has something to do with the death of my old self going into a rebirth or something. Maybe it represents skeletons in the closet.

Day 2 of the search
Angela Shelton in California

This is my crew's first official day on the road together. Yesterday was spent driving as far as we could until it got dark. We're 300 miles out of Los Angeles, and I have two women, two men, an RV, and myself to attend to. Giovanni is my soundman. Gallo is my cameraman. Chantal is my oldest friend—I've known her since I was 15. Sylvia was a production assistant on a friend's TV show. She jumped at the chance to come along when I told her I needed someone to drive. All of my crewmembers said that they wanted to get out of Los Angeles for the summer. Now I just have to keep them paid and fed for the next 60 days. I have no idea how I'm going to do that. The money I received from investors paid for the RV rental and will cover food for maybe one-fourth of the trip. But I keep hearing the Angela Sheltons in my head telling me to keep going and it will all work out.

None of us really knows what we're doing except for Giovanni. He's done sound on lots of movies before, and I keep hearing him say under his breath that this is going to be a circus. He wanted his own space, so I appointed the lazy chair in the RV just for him. It reminds me of having to keep my dad happy at all times to avoid his blowing up. I file those thoughts away though; I have a movie to make. I can't start thinking about my father. I've already told poor Sylvia that she can't drive. The nervous look on her face when she first stepped into this monster motor home alerted me to the fact that I can never let her behind the wheel. I should have thought about that before. Of course I should have thought about a lot of things, but I'm trusting that somehow everything will fall into place. Gallo reviewed the map with me and helped me establish a route that will save the most time and money. We're going in one big wobbly circle around the country, heading first toward Washington State.

My crewmembers looked shocked when I picked them up yesterday. They still can't believe we're actually doing this. I can't believe we are either. I especially can't believe I'm on the way to meet our first Angela Shelton. I pulled over to rearrange the RV to make everyone happy and suggested we film something just to get into the swing of things. I went to the pay phone and started calling the Angelas on my list that had never called me back. I tried one in Alabama. She said she'd be into seeing us but might not be home because she had softball practice. I found that amusing. Then I tried the Angela that was about an hour away just to see if she'd answer the phone, and she did. She told us to come to her office and she'd have coffee with us.

I almost swallowed my gum. I don't know why I'm so nervous. I think this is a good idea, but to be honest I'm not sure what to say to these women. I'm an actress and a writer and I even started working on a one-woman show. But faced with this project, I'm daunted. I'm unsure and nervous about what I'm doing. It feels like I want some kind of validation from my fellow females. This all started with me opening my big mouth. Now after speaking to so many of the women, a part of me wants to see how I measure up. I want to know how I'm doing.

We pull up to Angela Shelton's office, and I put on a big smile to hide my beating heart as we walk through the front door. She owns an insurance business with her husband. The building is under construction at the moment. She laughs when she comes into the lobby and sees us. I wonder if she can tell that I have no idea what I'm doing. We grin at each other. She gets coffee for my crew and snickers with her husband about being a movie star for a day as Gallo follows her around with the camera. She swears that she wants out of the insurance business and that her offices are about to change.

"I'll give you a tour and show you where all this construction is going to lead. It will be amazing. We've waited a long time for this." My crew and I follow her underneath the plastic-lined wall. "I don't want to do insurance anymore." She waves her hand at the room as if to shoo it all away. Then she smiles, happy with how it's transforming. She looks around the room with pride. "You know you spend all this time raising kids, and then they grow up. Now that the last one is leaving home, my husband and I get to have that time when we remember why we got married in the first place." She giggles. She's adorable.

"Have you been married a long time?"

"Twenty-one years." Holy mackerel, I think to myself. I wonder how in the world a person manages that. I'm the only product of nine marriages. My mother has been married five times now, and my father has been married four times last I heard. Neither one of them has had other kids. They've married people with kids, so I've been the oldest, the youngest, and the only child. And I haven't seen many marriages that have worked out in my life. It's refreshing to see Angela Shelton so happy in her marriage. "It works because we are best friends," she answers, reading my mind. "I was married once before to a man who believed in the tradition of a woman being barefoot, pregnant, and serving food. That was a totally different life, a different culture. Let me tell you, it's much more fun to live with my best friend." You can tell Angela and her husband have a good time together just by how they smile at each other.

"This is probably going to be our future," Angela says as she leads us through the rest of the building. "This is going to be our office, and two retail stores will be up in front, and then this is going to be a Kinship office, and upstairs will be office suites."

"What's a Kinship office?" I ask innocently.

"Kinship is the foster care and adoption nonprofit," she says. I stare at her. Did I hear that correctly? Foster care? The memory of my childhood floods over me as Angela Shelton points out her future. I feel tears well up way before she's done explaining how the foster care system works. I already know how it works. Angela notices me discreetly wipe a tear away.

"I was in a foster home," I explain. "It was horrible. They starved us. They would literally starve us." I have a flash memory of my foster mother and her skinny fireman husband. Angela looks at me, potentially waiting for more. I'm not sure I want to go into it, but her sweet nature makes me comfortable enough to talk. "The department of social services removed me and my stepsister from my dad's house and put us in a foster home. Our foster mother was a stay-at-home mom, but she was awful. And she was married to a fireman. They had one child of their own. They would feed him in front of us but then not feed us. It was bad."

"They really starved you?"

"Yeah, she would do things like make a huge pot of spaghetti and dish out an adult plate for her 5-year-old son and spoon out a little bite for me and my stepsister on small salad plates. Of course her son would take two or three bites and not eat his. He was 5. My stepsister and I would be finished in a second. Our foster mother would then take the rest of her son's plate and the entire pot and throw it into the trash right in front of us."

"That's awful. Why were you taken out of your home?"

"Um. I come from a home of incest." Angela's face becomes serious. I think her look of concern is what upsets me the most. I take a deep breath and try not to cry. This is supposed to be about her, not me. "It's so weird. I can talk about my dad all the time, but I can't talk about that foster home. It was horrible. It's so funny that you're renting space to a foster care nonprofit. It's great." I look around the room as Angela reaches over and hugs me. Over her shoulder I notice a dumpster against the outside of her building. Spray painted across the wall behind the dumpster is the phrase "Every child needs a family." It inspires more tears.

"But that was the only foster home you were in?"

"Yeah."

"Well, good, they got you out of there."

"Yeah, we only had to be there during the family court mess. They put my stepsister and me together in that foster home though, thankfully. You know, I don't even remember how long we were in there; I think it was three months. Maybe it was six months. It's weird. I feel like my brain blocked that memory out because it was so traumatic. But we had to live there while my dad went to trial. Well, it wasn't really a trial. He had to go to a hearing in family court. He was a child molester." Damn, I'm just laying it on this lady. Her face is so genuine and sweet that I can't help myself and the words pour out of me. Angela sighs and nods her head tenderly. "That was back around 1979. Back then they only worried about taking the kids out of the home. They didn't think once a pedophile, always a pedophile. So it was just a family hearing, a custody battle. Not a trial. But I had to go into foster care because my dad had full custody of me. He had fought my mom for it. That's a child-molester tactic to look like the superhero parent. But after the hearing my mom got custody back."

"He didn't go to jail?" Everyone always asks that question, and it's always weird to explain that my father molested all of us and nothing ever happened to him.

"No. There wasn't a real trial. There wasn't a jury or anything. My mom and my stepbrother and stepsister's real dad decided not to press criminal charges. Both of their lawyers urged them not to and said it was better to just deal with it in family court so they didn't have to put three kids in front of a jury. They didn't want to subject us to more abuse. They said it was the only case they'd seen that involved the whole family. One of the lawyers told my mom that if it did go to trial that it would become a miniseries on TV once the press got word of it. My mom and my stepsister and stepbrother's real father listened to their lawyers and didn't press charges. It was up to them. They didn't even ask us." Angela sighs. I wonder if I'm freaking her out. "I bet it would have been on TV though. I mean it wasn't like my father was sneaking into the little girl's room like you hear about most child molesters doing. It involved the whole family. My stepmother was opening the door for us to go into the bedroom with him. And then my brother was molesting us also. It was like a . . . um . . ."

"A lifestyle?" Angela finishes my sentence for me.

"Yes, a lifestyle." I have a memory of the last house we lived in, the A-frame. I can see it looming across the street from the lake. I can feel myself at 8 years old curling my toes up in the puke green shag carpet in the hallway outside of my dad's bedroom. I know he's in there with my sister. I come back to reality and look around Angela Shelton's office. "I think it's awesome that you're an Angela Shelton and you're renting out space to a foster care company. I mean it's just . . ." Angela reaches over and hugs me again. She can tell that I'm about to start crying again.

"It's OK. It's OK," she reassures me.

"Thanks," I peep out. "It just makes me so sad. It was such a horrible, horrible time in my life."

"But if you hadn't had that time, you wouldn't be where you are now."

"That's right." We smile at each other.

"It must have given you a lot of strength. And whatever happens, there's a reason for it even though it's difficult."

"I believe that too. Everything happens for a reason." We nod at each other. "Out of the 32 Angela Sheltons I've spoken with at this point, the ones that called me back anyway . . ." Angela grins and looks at the ground. I wave off the fact that she was one who didn't return my call. "So many of them have told me that they've been raped, beaten, or molested." Angela looks up. Her face is very serious.

"It's good that you bring that up, that you talk about it. It's a real problem in our society. It goes on because no one wants to talk about it. I never experienced anything like that. But whether it happened to me or not, it is happening. My mom died when I was 10. That was hard. Then my dad remarried three times after that. I did have a bizarre stepmother who locked me out of the house, but that was it. And one time a neighbor boy left me on the roof and I had to jump down," she adds and giggles. "But just because that kind of abuse didn't happen to me doesn't mean it isn't happening. Look at what you just said about the Angela Sheltons, and a person's name doesn't have to be Angela Shelton either. You're making a statement by doing this movie. You're revealing something big with this. Boy, I wish I was going on the road with you. I wish I had your balls."

I wonder if she would say that if she knew that I didn't know what the hell I'm doing. I like the fact that she's telling me what my movie is about. I wonder if she's right.

"It's good that you show women how other women are doing and what we're all going through. We need to learn new ways. We need guidance. That's why when I'm teaching my boys, I make sure that they're treating women with respect and having their own self-esteem and not victimizing anyone. That has to be taught to them."

I love Angela Shelton. I wish someone had taught my dad how not to victimize people like Angela is teaching her sons.

"What do you think helped you the most in your life?" I ask her. "What do you think kept you from experiencing any abuse, if there is a way to avoid it?"

Angela moves her coffee cup around in her hand, thinking. "My sisters. I had older sisters who really looked out for me and gave me strength. I learned a lot from them."

I only had an older stepsister for the five years that I lived with my dad. Maybe the Angela Sheltons can be like big sisters to me, coaching me in my life. I feel like that's already happening just from the ones I've talked with on the phone. Angela grins at me like she knows what I'm thinking. "You're doing a good job. This movie is going to help a lot of women."

Angela Shelton hugs me before I climb up the steps of the motor home to join my crew. I feel numb. I didn't expect to be confronted with my past so soon. I figured at some point during this trip I was going to tell my story, but I assumed it would be in North Carolina where it happened. We're not even out of California, and I'm already faced with my childhood trauma. My crew and I drive out of Angela's town, and half of me wants to turn around and go back to Los Angeles and forget this whole idea.

1980

"Angie," Miss Denis called out after she read the note in her hand. I was 8 years old. Miss Denis was my favorite teacher. She looked concerned. I figured that I must be in trouble. A teacher's aide had just handed her a note. Miss Denis looked at the note and then at me again as the teacher's aide left the room. She motioned for me to come to her desk. I made my way up to her as slowly as I could.

"The principal needs to talk to you, honey." She handed me a hall pass and put her hand on my shoulder like she was never going to see me again. I imagined the principal's paddle. What had I done? The walk to the principal's office was a long one. Everyone was in class so I was completely alone in the hall. I held onto my pass and made the long trek to the other end of the school. My dollar sneakers squeaked against the linoleum. I slowed down when I could see the principal's door. If I was going to get paddled, I was going to take my time. It reminded me of living with my dad. He beat us whenever he got the inkling. He didn't have to have a reason, and if he had one, it didn't have to make any sense. I took a deep breath and swallowed hard when I reached the principal's door. It opened into a waiting area. There on the bench outside the principal's private office sat my 10-year-old stepsister, Lisa. She looked like she'd seen a ghost. I wanted to know what was going on. Before I could ask her anything, two ladies stepped into my view. I had never seen them before, but they looked at me like they knew me.

"Hello there, you must be Angie. I'm Ms. Ford, and this is Ms. Lemons." She nodded toward the lady standing next to her. They both smiled down at me. I wondered where the principal was. I wondered if my stepsister had done something wrong.

"We're social workers," they explained. I didn't know what a social worker was.

I looked past them at Lisa's pale face and suddenly had a surge of fear that these ladies knew about my dad. I had to protect him. He didn't mean it. He was just teaching us. It was sex education in the home, he said. He was going to be mad if I said anything. I hoped that Lisa hadn't said anything. I didn't want to get in trouble. I didn't want my dad to get in trouble either.

"We'd like to talk to you about your dad," one of the ladies said, and my whole world stopped.

Dream Journal—May 4, 2001

I dreamed that I was a little kid riding a tricycle. I was pedaling down a highway pulling the 33-foot-long RV behind me. I was pushing as hard as I could, but I was only moving the huge vehicle an inch at a time. I wake up tired and relieved that the dream wasn't real. Then I realize I am inside the RV. I can't sleep now. Every time I close my eyes I hear the squeak of the tricycle wheels.

Day 3 of the search
Somewhere in Oregon

"I'm not sure what you're up to or what you want from me, but I'm hiding my credit cards," the Angela Shelton in Washington State warns me when I call to tell her I'm on my way. She reminds me that she lives in a secure community in case I have any ideas about robbing her. I assure her that I'm only coming to talk. I want to know how women are doing, even the paranoid ones who think this idea is stupid. I stop to get gas on the way. I go to the pump and watch the money flow into the huge RV tank. I hope this movie sells so I can pay all these bills. My credit card is already feeling the weight.

"You know about the power of rocks?" I turn to see a woman next to me going through a vast collection of rocks in the bed of her pickup truck. I smile at her. "Check this one out," the woman says and hands me a rock filled with green sparkles and black valleys. I turn it over in my hand. "You can have it if you want."

"Thanks." I drop it into my pocket and wonder if my crew will accept rocks as pay.

"Where are you all headed?"

"Um," I pause, watching the gas gauge roll past $50. I wonder if I should tell her the short version or the long version. "We're making a movie, a documentary."

"Oh, that's cool. What's it about?"

"Um, well, my name is Angela Shelton, and I'm traveling around the country to meet all the other Angela Sheltons."

"Oh my God. That's so funny."

"Yeah, I thought so too in the beginning, but then I started calling them and found out that a lot of them have been raped, beaten, or molested; half of them so far actually."

The woman's face freezes. Maybe I should have kept my mouth shut. I can tell from the expression on her face that one of the three has happened to her too. "You're doing a good thing, you know. This needs to be talked about. Nobody talks about this stuff."

"I know. Even some of the Angelas don't want to talk about it. Some have canceled on me already."

"Well, they should talk. The statistics are all wrong; it happens a lot more than people think."

"I know. It happened to me too."

"Me three." We share an apologetic grin like we understand the pain of each other's struggle. "And my daughter, and also my brother. He was molested too."

"Oh my God. All by the same person?"

"No, my uncle molested my brother, a guy at school raped me, and a neighbor molested my daughter." I sigh as the woman with the rocks continues. She seems so grateful to be able to purge. "I had always prepared her for what to do if something like that should happen to her, but I hadn't prepared myself, as a mother, for what I should do if it should happen to her."

We both stand there staring at each other. My pump clicks to the end, and I pull the nozzle out and put it back into its cradle. All of a sudden this rock woman starts jumping up and down like a giddy child. "It's so good that you're out talking about this! I'm so excited about what you're doing! I tried to talk about this epidemic after it happened to my daughter, but so many people thought I was crazy. I'm so excited about what you're doing. It's about time we break the silence about this."

"Do you want a T-shirt?" I ask, not knowing what else to say. "We have *Searching for Angela Shelton* T-shirts."

"Oh, yes!" she calls out likes she's on a game show. "I can't believe I just met you while you were pumping gas."

"I know, right? Life is funny." I fondle the rock in my pocket and have an idea. "Actually, do you want to be interviewed? I mean, your name isn't Angela Shelton, but you're a woman in America and surveying women is what this is all about."

"Yes! Yes! Yes!" she blurts out without any pause. I go and get Gallo and the rest of the crew. We get the equipment ready, and I start to interview this woman named Lori right in front of the gas station where I met her.

"So what happened?" I ask her.

"My daughter, when she was 5 years old, was sexually molested by a 13-year-old. It was a family that everybody thought was so respectful, and it wasn't. But we need to teach others how to talk about it and to get it out. Because if you don't get it out, then you keep on pushing it down. And when you keep on pushing it down, it spreads. It becomes an epidemic when you're quiet. I knew how to calm my daughter and tell her that it was not her fault, but I didn't know what to do for myself," Lori admits. "I was a wreck. When I went to the police, they said, 'Why are you crying? He didn't penetrate.' " She and I both make a face at how ridiculous that sounds. "He stuck his thing down her throat. Now if that isn't penetration, I don't know what is. I mean I don't know what you think penetration is, but it was a violation, and it violated me as well as my daughter. And the way I was handled in the system is so messed up." I think about my experience with the system. I'm grateful my social workers were nice and that they put my stepsister and me together in foster care. "But we need to teach people like you're doing. We need to get out there and say, 'It's OK, and it's not your fault.'" Lori tightens her grip on my hands and looks me straight in the eye. "What you're doing is great." I hope she's right. I don't feel too great at this moment.

"It's weird. It's making me really look at my own past. I started this project to make a movie that inspired women. I wasn't expecting to talk about this subject over and over, but it keeps coming up. And here you are pumping gas next to me."

"It's coming up because it's supposed to. Everything happens for a reason."

"Yeah. But after a while it's just too much."

"Yeah, but like I said, we need to talk about it. I was raped when I was 13. He was a senior who offered me a ride home so I didn't have to take the bus. I thought it was cool to ride with a senior, so I went. I got into his car. I'd love to tell all the girls today to stay on the bus. Don't trust older boys who want to give you things. He drove me 15 miles from my house and told me I'd have to do it with him or he would leave me there on the road. I did it because I was scared and didn't see a way out. That's how I lost my virginity."

"Good God. I'm so sorry."

"And I didn't tell anybody. I just kept quiet because I felt so stupid for getting a ride from him in the first place. My mom was so mad that I was late coming home too, so I kept quiet. See, my brother had already told about his abuse at that point, and nobody believed him. So I knew to stay quiet." I feel like I'm going to throw up.

"You said your uncle molested your brother?"

"Yeah. And my uncle was such an upstanding guy too, so nobody believed my brother. The guy who raped me, same thing. He was so well liked that I figured nobody would believe me, so I didn't bother telling."

"So is my dad. He's charming and manipulative. A salesman."

"Yes! That's exactly it, manipulative."

"And my dad was the candy man. He filled up the candy machines at the front of the grocery stores. He had a van full of all that candy. He owned an arcade too."

"Oh my God, Angela."

I'm thinking about her uncle instead of my dad when I say, "What an ass."

"I know. And you know what's really messed up?" I wait for her to tell me that the wife knew it all along and did nothing about it. "My brother started doing drugs."

"Well, that figures. What else are you going to do when you're in hell?"

"Yeah, while the rapist walks free. My brother was the one who went to drugs and couldn't deal. He ended up in prison. And it all started with my uncle raping him. My uncle was an awful man. He denied it the whole nine yards. The entire family protected him. That's what happens with these men. They're so upstanding in our society that people protect them. You can't believe that the nice man is hurting children. It makes me sick.

You know how it is. And they get away with it because of that too. My brother killed himself in jail," Lori tosses out and makes my heart jump. "My uncle molested and sodomized my brother, and then my brother is the one who kills himself. How messed up is that?" She looks off into the distance.

"Really messed up." I stare off with her at the cars passing on the highway.

"My uncle died in a car accident not too long after that." She turns to me with a smile.

"Good. I have no sympathy for people who rape children," I tell her.

"Me neither. Did you ever talk to your dad?"

"Um," I stall. Can't I just hate child molesters and leave my dad out of it? "I wrote him a letter about it, but he never responded."

"Figures. They never want to take responsibility." We stand there for a moment before she gets excited again. "You all are doing such a good thing. I love what you're doing." She looks around at my small crew, all of whom are in tears at this point. "You need to do this, Angela. You need to do this. You're being led. You're being guided. You need to trust in that."

After hugging me and holding my hands firmly again, Lori says goodbye and heads toward the mini-mart connected to the gas station. The crew and I spend the next couple moments getting situated in the RV before we continue on our way. Lori and her stories have stunned all of us. I want to leave. I want to start driving again and not think about any of this. There's a knock on the RV door. I open it, grateful for the distraction, and find Lori standing there.

"I'm so glad you haven't left yet. I just had to come back and give you this." She hands me a pin shaped like a heart with a peace sign in the middle. "It's a peace-of-heart pin, like peace in heart. I've had it since I was like 14 or something." My eyes start to well up with tears. "I just want you to have peace of heart because you just gave me peace of heart. You really did. Everything happens for a reason, and I just want you to know that this is the best day of my whole life. I don't know what made you come here, but I just wanted to say thank you so much." She reaches in to hug me, and I hug her back. I clip the peace-of-heart pin in my hair. I will wear it every day of this trip.

February 2001—three months before searching
Preproduction, Los Angeles

I'm sitting here holding a list of Angela Sheltons. There's one in almost every state. My long list of Angelas is highlighted in places and has x marks through the ones with disconnected numbers. I'm taking notes by the ones I speak to, but I can already tell that I'm going to need a binder to organize all these women.

I get a lump in my throat with every new Angela I call. I feel apprehensive and nervous about cold-calling them, but then I pick up the phone quickly and hope for the best. I just got off the phone with one in North Carolina who was really bitter about this project. She told me that she had a gun and it was loaded and she wasn't about to tell anyone about what happened to her in her life. I just apologized and wished her well and hung up quickly. I make a note by her name to not call her again. There are a few Angelas in California that I can hopefully see on the way up to Washington. I get a kick out of the one in Washington. She says this idea is so stupid. She made me laugh out loud. I hope that the rest of the Angelas return my calls. I have a long list of Angelas in Oklahoma, but none of them have called me back yet. Three Angela Sheltons are in South Carolina. That's where my dad lives. One lives right in his town too. I haven't called her yet. It makes me nervous. She is one I hope has a disconnected phone. I would prefer to avoid my dad's town. I call the Angela farthest away from my dad.

"I am extremely skeptical," she alerts me. "What are your credentials? Who is your producer?"

"I think HBO is going to do it."

"Well, I will need to speak to the producer. I have never heard of you."

"I'm just the filmmaker Angela Shelton surveying other Angela Sheltons." She's silent. I can feel her disbelief through the phone line. I flip through my stack of Angelas. "I've spoken to almost 30 so far, and you want to know what's sad? Fourteen have been raped, beaten, or molested."

"That doesn't surprise me. I was beaten by my husband."

"Really? Now that is 15 out of 30."

"Well, I'll be traveling during the time you're doing your project, so I won't be in the country anyway. If you want me involved, you'll have to have your producer call me."

She hangs up. I sit here wishing I had a big fancy producer. I call the other Angela in South Carolina, the one who isn't in my dad's town.

"That happened to me too," she says quietly after I tell her about all of the different Angelas who share pasts of abuse.

"What part?"

"All of it. Except I was raped more than once," she adds like it is no big deal.

That's 16 out of 32 women now who have experienced trauma.

"I'm sorry." I don't know what to say. I want to know more, but I don't want to be insensitive. I flip through my stack of Angelas in amazement. I can't believe so many women have been victims. Well, actually I can believe it. My mother, my aunt, my best friend, my cousin, my stepsister, my ex-boyfriend have all told me stories about their abuse.

"I was almost raped the first time when I was 13," Angela continues without my pressing. "Well, no, I guess the first time was when I was 8." Before I can let that sink in she continues, "I was almost abducted when I was 8 too."

"So was I," I pipe in. "What is it with that age?"

"Freaks," she says. I think about my dad. He doesn't look like a freak. He looks like any other fat man with a beard. "I have three kids now," Angela Shelton tells me. "I watch them like a hawk. My daughter has medical problems. We have to go to Charleston all the time for the doctor."

"Charleston?" I get a sinking feeling in the pit of my stomach.

"Yeah, pretty city."

"My dad lives in Charleston now."

"Oh yeah?"

"Yeah, he's a child molester."

"Oh. He did that to you too?" she says.

"Yeah."

"Crap. Mine won't talk about it. I tried to confront him two years ago, but the bastard wouldn't listen to a word I said."

"So you were molested too?"

"Yeah, but my mom left him when I was 8."

"There's that age again." We both laugh because we don't know what else to do. "I went to live with my mom when I was 8 too," I tell her.

"Oh yeah? Did your mom take your dad back when you were 11 like mine did?"

"No."

"He even beat the crap out of her and she went back. Those were the days. Now he's with a new girlfriend who has kids."

"Oh my God."

"Yeah." I can hear her moving around her house. It sounds like she's cleaning.

"Did you end up marrying someone abusive? I know that happens a lot."

"Which time? I ran away when I was 16. I was with a guy who beat me up pretty bad. I thought I was free of that, but then I married a guy when I was 17 and he beat me up too."

"Why'd you stay with them?" She's silent. I hear her kids running in and out of the house. A screen door slams. I make some assumptions. "You said your father beat your mother?"

"Oh yeah, all the time. It scared us kids half to death."

"That's so awful. Are you with a good guy now? The father of your kids?"

"Um . . . yeah, he's hit me a few times before though." I'm actually a little nervous to go see this Angela. What if some gun-toting Southern guy comes after me with a sawed-off shotgun, ready to shoot the woman who stole his wife's name? "But he promised he wouldn't do it again." I feel so bad for this Angela Shelton, and yet I want to strangle her at the same time for her denial. She's doing what her mother did.

"Jeez." I hope that I can convince her to leave once I get there. "And you were almost raped before that too?" I leave the subject of her abusive husband for a minute.

"Oh yeah. I was raped when I was 16 pretty bad. Then I was almost raped at 13, but I got away that time."

"Jesus. How'd you get away?"

"This guy tried to drag me into the bushes on the way home from school. I fought him off and ran home."

"Did you tell? Did he get caught?"

"I told my dad. I knew what the guy looked like and everything, and he went looking for him."

"Oh, that's awesome. Did he kick his ass?"

"No. He took him out for a beer."

"What?!"

"He took him out for a beer."

"I heard you, but are you kidding me?"

"No. It made me sick too."

"I hate to be rude and I don't mean to be, but do you have super-low self-esteem? I mean how could you have any self-esteem when your own father takes your rapist out for a beer? That's seriously messed up. I hope you know how messed up that is."

"Yeah, but we all go through things. Life is hard and then you die, right?"

"How are you doing now?"

"I get by. I was in an institution for a while. I have sleeping disorders. I'm manic-depressive. You know. I have to take medication."

"That makes me crazy that you now have to pay for the abuse that others did to you. You're the one labeled crazy."

"That's right. It's the price we pay for living in a man's world. They get away with a lot and then we protect them, right? But who knew I'd be in a movie?"

"Yeah. I can't wait to meet you."

"I'll take you and your crew down to Savannah."

"Oh, cool. I've never been there before. I've always wanted to go."

"It's a real pretty city like Charleston."

"Yeah, Charleston is pretty." I wonder if I can avoid going there. I don't want to think about my dad or the pretty city he lives in. I wonder if Angela Shelton's dad was a charmer like mine. I bet her husband hides behind the mask of the good guy too. I have a fantasy of saving this Angela Shelton. I draw a big star next to her name on my list.

1983

When I was only 8 I managed to run away from some weird guy who tried to pull me into his car. He had no idea that I already knew what he had planned. When I was 11 though, I had my friend Kat with me. It had been a few years since I had lived with my dad. I was living with my mom and her fourth husband in Greenville, South Carolina. We were already pretty good at spotting creeps. Her dad was a weirdo like mine. There was also a creep who drove up and down Kat's block pulling on his thingy and watching us play outside. We threw rocks at that guy. He wasn't as scary as this old lady in the movie theater though.

Kat and I went to see *The Color Purple*. I'd already seen it twice, but I wanted to go again. Plus it was so hot outside that the movie theater was the best place to cool off. Kat's mom dropped us off, and her dad was supposed to pick us up. We got candy and went to search for seats. I liked the middle, so we scooted all the way down the row. The movie started, and we were both into it right away even though I knew most of the words already. We weren't too far into the movie when I felt breathing against my neck. I turned like a shot, and there was an old lady in the row behind us, whispering to me. She was weird. I couldn't understand what she wanted. She wasn't making any sense.

"What?" I whispered back.

"You are two nice little girls. It's so good to see you. Such nice girls." I wanted to tell her to shut up, but I just grinned, nodded, and turned back to the movie.

I didn't notice her making her way down our aisle until she was already halfway toward us. She was dressed in a sad old lady dress, clutching a bag, and her hair was pinned up in a bun. She sat down next to me. But I didn't say anything. There were plenty of other seats around. I wasn't sure why she picked us to sit next to. Then she put her hand on my knee. I turned to her quickly, but before I could say anything, she started telling me some bizarre story.

"I used to have a little girl like you. But she's in heaven now. She's no longer with us. I sure am lonely now. I sure am." I just nodded at her uncomfortably and tried to turn back to the movie. I looked down at her hand on my knee until she lifted it off. "I'd just love for you to come home with me for just a little while. I could show you her room. She was such a nice child. And you two are such nice little girls." Kat leaned forward as if on cue to check out what was going on next to me. I turned to her wide-eyed to express how creepy this lady was.

"I'm really sorry about your kid," I whispered. "But we're watching the movie."

"Oh, I'm so sorry. I just thought you'd be a nice girl and help out an old lady. I only wanted a moment of your time. I'm so lonely, you see."

I turned and gave Kat a look, and she lifted up from her chair and scooted to the other end of the aisle. I felt totally guilty for just leaving an old lady there like that, but *The Color Purple* was my favorite movie, and I had no intention of going home with some creepy granny. Kat and I made it farther down the aisle and sat down. I turned to look at the lady apologetically, but she was gone. A few minutes later I felt her hot breath on the side of my face again. She was behind me. I bolted out of my seat, up the aisle, and out the door so fast I don't know what hit me. I spotted a theater attendant and told him a weird old lady was following us around in the theater. He pulled his mini flashlight out of his pocket and told me to follow him. He went into the theater and down to our row, aiming his light on the ground as we walked. Kat was there but the old lady was gone. The attendant told me to sit down with my friend and he'd look through the theater. I made my way back to Kat. She hadn't seen anything. She was engrossed in the film. I was paying more attention to the theater attendant who was going up and down the aisles scanning for the granny. She had disappeared.

I tried to forget about it, and halfway through the film I was successful. But once the movie was over and Kat and I were leaving, Kat brought up the creepy old lady. We wondered what that was all about as we moved outside into the bright sun to wait for Kat's dad to pick us up. As we stood there waiting for our pupils to adjust to the afternoon light, we both saw her at the same time. Granny was making her way across the parking lot, but she was no granny. It was a man dressed up like an old lady. We could see it so plainly in the sunlight. Kat and I both looked at each other in horror. I felt sick, remembering his hand on my knee and the invitation to his house. Kat and I were mortified, thinking about what that granny man had planned for little girls like us. I thought about the dead girl he had mentioned. Kat's dad finally pulled up. I wondered who was worse but didn't say anything. We told Kat's dad the story as he pulled out into the street. He kept asking for us to point the man out. He said we should report it, but the granny man had disappeared. I wondered what Kat's dad would say about our reporting him for what he did to Kat. But I kept my mouth shut and my eyes peeled for creeps disguised as little old ladies.

Day 4 of the search
Angela Shelton in Washington State

"Just don't ask me any personal questions," the rich Angela Shelton says.

"Asking personal questions is the whole point. I'm surveying women in America. Aren't you curious to know about other women in America?"

"Well, after we hung up the first time, you did pique my curiosity. I was thinking I wanted to know what color hair they all had, what color eyes, are they tall, thin, what they did for a living, their backgrounds. You got me interested. But I still hid my credit cards." I look around her gated community that sits on the edge of a golf course. I figure if you have money like this you have to assume everyone is trying to get it.

"I don't want your money. I just want to talk to you. Of course if you'd like to invest in the movie, that would be great too," I joke. She doesn't think it's funny.

"So you think this is actually going to be a movie?" her husband, Dave, asks as we unload our equipment and he and Angela sign releases.

"Yes, I do."

"If people want their $7 back at the movies, we're not liable, are we?"

"No," I assure him, kind of insulted. He reminds me of the people in Hollywood who told me I was nuts to do this after I didn't receive funding. I decided not to listen to any naysayer and kept moving forward, and I'm not about to let any husband of any Angela Shelton make me second-guess myself. I just smile at him.

Once we're situated on her patio overlooking the ninth hole, I ask the rich Angela Shelton my broad questions about who she is, where she's been, and where she's going. "I'm nothing special. Certainly nobody that anybody wants to hear about in a movie." I try to explain that we all have a story, but she doesn't buy it. She has two kids and a husband and that's it. "Something tragic just happened to my daughter-in-law, but you can't record that part. I'm not talking about that." She sits in silence for a moment. I don't know what to ask her. I watch some golfers walk past her backyard on their way to the ninth hole. "Did you see that movie *Pay It Forward*?" she asks. I wonder if she's trying to avoid her life by changing the subject.

"No, I didn't, but I heard about it."

"Well, the end is awful, but the message is great."

"What's that? To pay things forward?"

"Yes. You have to pay it forward, pass on the good things that happen to you."

"That's a good message."

"I truly believe that everything happens for a reason, and that there is a force out there. I don't know whether it's God, or Spirit, or whatever, but I believe that it's directing you."

"I believe that," I say. She and I finally have something in common.

"Good, because you're an Angie Shelton," she says. We smile at each other.

"What did you think when I first called you?"

She looks at me like I'm crazy. "I thought, why? Why would you do that? I mean it just seems pointless to me. But I will admit that you got me interested—I'll say that much. I don't know if I'd go see a documentary like this, but you did get me interested."

"You might if you were in it."

"It depends on what you put in it."

"So far, to be honest, half of the Angelas have been abused, raped, beaten, or molested."

"Well, none of those things ever happened to me."

"Not all women are abused," I assure her, trying to put her at ease. I want to tell her that she's not tainted. She's not like me.

"I will admit that I grew up really poor though."

"So did I." I peruse her landscaped yard. "But you have money now."

"Yes, money is always better. But it's not the most important thing. But it is better." I think about my dwindling bank account. "This is the good life. I do get bored sometimes though." She surveys the surrounding golf course. "I wonder if I should volunteer somewhere or something. But I refuse to work. My husband says I'm a leisure technologist."

"You've been married a long time?"

"Thirty-one years."

"Wow. That reminds me of the California Angela. She's the second oldest. You're the oldest one so far at 48."

"Don't tell me that! I'll get up and leave right now."

"Come on, age is beautiful."

"Spoken by a young woman," she scoffs.

"How old were you when you got married?" I want to move on to more personal things.

"Eighteen."

"Wow. Eighteen. Can I ask you some personal questions?"

"Sure, you can ask."

"Does that mean that you lost your virginity to him?"

She laughs uncomfortably. "Yes."

"How is that? I mean, if he was the first and only man you were with, do you feel that you missed out on anything by not exploring more?" I glance at her husband in the kitchen watching us.

"No, it's completely the opposite. I feel like I gained something, like we beat the odds." I can see her beating the odds on many levels. I think of all the women who, like me, didn't have the opportunity to give their virginity away.

Losing my virginity is the best way to describe my experience. The best-looking boy at school asked me out when I was 14 and he was 17. He drove a red Camero. I hated that car, but it was one of the reasons he was so popular. He took me out for some food and then to the beach. It was dark by then. He laid a blanket out and suggested that we sit on it. We sat down and started making out, and before I knew it he was up my shirt and down my pants. I was so shocked that this popular boy would want to do this with me that I didn't even fight him. I thought he was just touching me down there. It was weird but I was already out too late as it was, so I didn't urge him to take me home. He wrestled with his pants, and before I could say anything I was losing my virginity. I didn't even know it was happening. I felt a twinge of pain, and there I was: a nonvirgin at 14. I thought he was a jerk. He got his pants on again and told me to fold up the blanket. At least he carried it back to his car. He pulled into a convenience store on the way to drop me off at my house. He pulled in and parked and turned to me.

"Do you have $2?" I looked at him, totally confused. Was I supposed to pay for this too? "I have to go in there and get my dad a Father's Day card. It's Father's Day already, you know. I need $2." He nodded toward the car clock and it was way past midnight. I handed him $2 and wondered how my mother was going to react when I got home. I could feel myself bleeding on his dumb Camero seat, but I didn't care about his car. I watched him inside buying a Father's Day card and realized that I had lost my virginity on Father's Day. I told my mother where I'd been when I came home. She was angry that I hadn't called her, but she just cried and cried when I told her the full story.

I turn toward the Washington State Angela and wonder what it would have been like to have been a virgin bride. "I am a troublemaker though," she tosses in, and I perk up, excited to hear about a saucy side of her.

"How so?"

"Oh, just not following the rules." She waves her hand, indicating the community she lives in. "I get in trouble all the time. I'm sure I'll get a letter about having your RV parked in front of our house because I didn't get it approved—things like that. Everyone is so uptight."

"Do you want me to write you a doctor's note or something?" She laughs.

"No, I'm used to getting in trouble. I handle it well," Angela assures me as her husband comes back outside. He brought golf clubs so we could hit in a few balls. Angela says that they are already in trouble, so we might as well take advantage of it. We play around, whacking balls. I'm a terrible shot. It's nice to goof around though, to add some humor to the trip.

"So you're just going around the country asking all of these Angela Sheltons the same questions?" Dave asks as he stands next to his wife.

"Yes, I want to survey women in America, and calling women who share my name is much easier than just knocking on random doors."

"What is the most common thing you've found so far?"

"That most of them have a past of rape, incest, or domestic violence, which says something about women in general, I think."

"Well, the only abuse that Angela has gone through is that she likes to be spanked." Angela hits him across the chest playfully.

"You don't need to share my secrets, Dave."

"She doesn't have any past like that, but you're saying all these other women do?"

"Not all, but most of the ones I've spoken to do, yes. And myself. I was also molested." They both look at me sideways.

"Oh," Dave sighs. "So that's why you're doing this." I don't know how to answer him. I wonder if I really am searching for myself.

"Not really. I was planning on writing some sort of theater piece around my story. This movie is about women. I hope to inspire women. I would love to show that we've come a long way. But when I started calling the Angelas and I shared who I am, my past, and where I'm going, they shared their stories. And there is a common thread of abuse. I'm told that when you make a documentary the story reveals itself through the process. You might be planning one thing and end up with something entirely different. My only real plan is to make the movie inspirational."

"You think it will end up on TV?" I want to scream at him, but I smile and nod instead.

"I hope so. That's the plan." The crew and I have to get going to start the long trek toward Kansas. I wish I had more time to spend with each Angela. This Angela and her husband seem amused by us and glad to see us go.

1980

"It is OK to talk to us. We're safe," one of the social workers assured me. "What else goes on in your house that you don't like?" I looked at my stepsister. Ms. Ford and Ms. Lemons stared at me expectantly. I said nothing. "What did you do before you went to the nudist colony?" They were trying a different angle. They were trying to get my stepsister and me to talk, but they weren't telling us what to say. We didn't know what they wanted. I hated it.

"Um," I paused and looked up at them. Something in my mind told me to tell them about my dad spreading my step-mother's legs and showing her off to us. I wondered if I should tell them how we had to rub my dad's thing until the white stuff came out. I told my brain to be quiet. I was worried that Daddy would get in trouble if I said anything. Daddy would be mad.

"Are you scared that your father will be mad at you if you tell us about what he does to you at home?" I shut my eyes, realizing they could read my mind.

"Yes."

"We will make sure that he can't hurt you anymore. You have our word." I wondered what that meant. "You can trust us. We will make sure that you're safe. What your father did was wrong."

"What about Steve? Where is Steve?" I asked.

"He's staying with Dad," Lisa piped in. "He told our dad what your dad does."

Her words stung me. This was all my fault. My dad was the abuser, not Lisa's. Steve had gone away for the summer to his real dad's house. We hadn't seen Steve in quite a while. He was supposed to come back home that summer but didn't. Maybe he told because he didn't want to come back to live with my dad anymore. My dad was the bad one. I felt like it was all my fault because I was my dad's only child.

"When your stepbrother told his real father, his real father called social services. That's us," Ms. Lemons explained. "That's why we're here talking to you. Our job is to keep you safe. We're going to take you and Lisa to a special home. You'll get to go to a new school and have a new place to stay. We're taking you there ourselves. Then we'll go meet with your parents and get some of your clothes and things."

I didn't want to go. Lisa looked relieved, but I was worried about my dad. "What happens to my dad?" Lisa looked at me like I was stupid. I thought maybe I was.

"We'll let him know that you're OK. Don't worry." I wondered if they were going to get us in trouble. I looked at Lisa again. We had told our secrets to two strangers. The social workers just nodded the whole time and took notes on their yellow pads.

"Everything is going to be OK." Ms. Ford put her arm around me. It didn't seem OK.

Day 5 of the search
Somewhere in Idaho

"My father doesn't remember anything," the alcoholic Angela mumbles and takes a breath like she's trying to suck that sentence back in. I have the phone cradled to my ear. I hear her open another beer. Damn, she drinks fast.

"Well, neither does mine if that helps you feel any better. I love how they conveniently don't remember anything."

"Well, no . . ." She pauses. I cradle the phone to my ear and stare at the full moon above us. "He has Alzheimer's," she says, and we both burst out laughing.

"Shoot, now he really doesn't remember anything." I stop laughing. I wonder how her father abused her and if she has ever dealt with it. I suspect she hasn't dealt with much. It's apparent that she hides her pain in a can. "Wow, that's hard. How is that for you? Are you going to therapy?"

"I can't afford therapy." She pauses for a long time and then whispers, "I'm fine." I wait for her to say more.

"You're fine?" I jump in sarcastically. "You're funny. You're always saying that you're nothing, that I shouldn't come see you, that you're nobody, but you're fine?" She chuckles. "If anything you're the number one Angela I need to meet."

"I don't know who you are, but I'm not pretty." I'm losing her; she's going into that mumbling drunken place she tends to go to after one too many. Maybe she's almost at the end of her case of beer. "I'm invisible really. I'm just lower than a dog."

"That's harsh."

"But I am. I'm lower than a dog."

"Who told you that?" She doesn't answer. She's crying.

"Just lower than a dog."

"Did your father tell you that?"

"Oh yes. Every day."

"Jesus." We sit there for a moment. I watch the road go by. Gallo is driving. Sylvia and Giovanni are asleep. Chantal files her nails. I can hear Angela light a cigarette and I wish I had one. "Angela, if you just told me that you're lower than a dog, aren't you just repeating what your father said to you?"

"Yeah."

"But that's not true. You shouldn't believe that. It's just a stupid lie some stupid man said to you. He doesn't get to label you like that. I don't care if it is your dad." She doesn't disagree with me. She just cries. "Is that why you drink?"

"Oh yeah."

"It's hard, you know. We all want to be loved."

"I know. God, I am so drunk right now."

"Have you ever been to AA or rehab?"

"Oh sure, many times," she snorts. Then she either hangs up or drops the phone. I don't know which. All I get is a dial tone.

March 2001—two months before the search
Preproduction, Los Angeles

I stare at the number for the Angela Shelton in my dad's town. I quickly dial her number before I lose my nerve. She answers, and I don't know what to say. I swallow hard and then go into my usual sales pitch about being a filmmaker and making a movie about women in America. She thinks I'm a telemarketer. So I start telling her about the various Angela Sheltons.

"That sounds neat. Is it OK if I wasn't originally a Shelton? That's my married name."

"That's totally fine. Many of the Angelas have Shelton as their married name. And I wasn't born a Shelton either."

"Were you adopted?"

"No, my father is a child molester, and I didn't want to carry his name."

"Oh. That makes sense."

"Actually he lives in your town. That's why I've held off on calling you for so long."

"Really? I should look him up. I'm going to school for criminal justice, and I'm tracking sexual predators." My stomach falls to my knees. "You should give me his name."

"What?"

"His name, since you changed yours. You should give me his name and I'll look him up on the offender list."

"No. No. I don't have his last name anymore. I chose Shelton." I wait for a moment and then tell Angela Shelton my dad's name and the street he lives on. "So how old are you? Are you married? I guess you just told me what you do for a living." I'm fumbling, trying to cover my main questions so I can make notes by her name.

"This is really a neat idea. Are you really coming here to make a movie?"

"Yep. I wanted to make one over the summer. I just want to see how we're all doing. And unfortunately half have been raped, beaten, or molested."

"That doesn't surprise me at all. Most of those crimes are never reported. Victims of those crimes usually feel that they're the only ones. It's good that you bring that up. And by the way, there are 400 registered child molesters here in the area by the beach alone. And those are just the registered ones. Can you believe it?"

"I bet my dad isn't registered. He never got caught, officially. It was only in family court."

"Well, I'll check up on him. You have no idea what he's been up to over the years. I have to get back to work, but I'll let you know what I find. And let me know when you're going to be here. I still can't believe this. Are you sure you're not a telemarketer?" I assure her again that I'm not, but I really wish I were one at the moment so I could hang up and never call again.

I have to go lie down.

1979

"I always wish you were my mom," my stepsister confided in my real mom. My mom smiled and hugged her as my stepsister climbed down from her lap. We were sitting together on a curb in a grocery store parking lot. I was just 7 years old and we were finishing lunch. My dad and my stepmother were standing just down the way, waiting for me to be done visiting with my mom.

My dad didn't let me see my mom much. One time when she came to visit me, he literally picked her up from the porch and threw her down the stairs. He was a really big man. My mom skidded across the walkway that led to the steps. Her arms were all bloody and her knees were scraped. We were both crying. I tried to see her from behind my dad, but he yelled at me to get back inside the house. I was glad when I was able to see her in public because my dad couldn't act like that. He put on his Mr. Perfect face. Lisa had run over to the curb where we sat because she liked my mom so much. My stepmother gave her a look, so she waved bye to my mom and went back to her real mother's side. I clung to my mom's neck.

"I want to go home with you, Mama."

"I know. I'm working on it. I have to get custody of you."

"Can't you just get it?"

"Your father has it right now, sweetie. It's complicated. We have to go to court, but I'm working on it." She looks down the way toward my dad and my stepmother. I wonder if I should tell her what my dad does at home. She touches my face and looks into my eyes. "We can meet in our dreams though, did you know that?" I didn't understand what she meant. "When you're wishing you were back with me, just come meet me in your dreams. We can see more of each other that way. Does that make it easier?"

"Yeah."

"That way we can be together in our dreams until we can be together in person again. We can both write our dreams down and make them come true."

Later that week I dreamed that I was walking on the beach with my mom.

Dream Journal—May 7, 2001

   I had a nightmare. I dreamed that I was trying to move the dead body in the body bag again I was trying to get it out of this dark house with dark corridors everywhere. I was so nervous about being found liquid was oozing out through the zipper on the bag The juices were all over my feet and hands. I tried not to vomit as I pulled the body out the door into the light I made it I couldn't unzip the bag to drain it I didn't want to see the face. I knew that the body in the bag was mine.

Day 6 of the search
Somewhere in Montana

I keep having flashbacks to my nightmare like I'm still in it. I'm grateful my crew and I are only driving today and won't meet any Angelas. We pull over to film an update of what's happened so far, but as soon as the camera starts rolling, I start crying. "I'm halfway between Washington and Kansas, and I'm not sure why I'm doing this. I know I'm making a movie but I'm in a weird spot. I keep thinking about how weird it was to meet that woman at the gas station." I fiddle with the peace-of-heart pin in my hair. "I keep thinking about her and all the Angelas. And I'm feeling lost. It's perfect that I'm in the middle of nowhere. I feel like that." I don't know what else to say, so I tell Gallo to shut the camera off.

We get back on the road and I decide to call the Angela in South Carolina who is living with her abusive husband and swears he won't hit her again. I want to remind her again that we're on our way. I have a fantasy of rolling up to her house in the motor home and saving her and her kids. I dial her number and the phone rings once. "At the customer's request, this number has been disconnected." Crap. I try again and get the same recording. I try information and get no listing for an Angela Shelton in her town. I try the same number again and again and get the same recording.

I picture Angela Shelton telling her husband that people from Hollywood are coming to make a movie about her. I picture her bragging about it to everyone. I picture him taking it badly, resorting back to his dumb rage, and removing the only access I have to her. I feel like a failure. I should have asked her for her address. I should have planned for this. All I have is her phone number and her story. I should have known this was going to happen.

"What's the matter?" Chantal asks because I can't hide the anxiety on my face.

"I just lost the Angela Shelton who needs me most."

"The alcoholic?"

"No, the one who lives with her abusive husband." Crap, crap, crap. I feel like throwing something. I feel like smacking myself. I had a plan. We were going to help her escape. That was part of the inspiration and empowerment of the movie. Now I'm a thousand miles from her with no access. I'm so stupid. I try the number again just for the hell of it and I hear the same recording again. I hang up before the computerized voice reminds me what an idiot I am. I go back to the RV bedroom and cry. I have failed, and it's only the sixth day. I'm alone in the room so I smack myself good and hard across the face for not getting Angela's address. I am so stupid. I lie on the bed as we move down the highway and pinch my leg until I bleed.

1980

I was 8 years old the first time I smacked myself. The court hearing was over, and my dad and stepmother were ordered to seek psychological counseling and my mother won full custody. Some man she used to date was a big real estate tycoon in Asheville, North Carolina, and he helped her buy a house. We had a new life and a new house together. My mom even had the kitchen remodeled so that half of it was my size. There was a little counter, little cabinets, and everything. She bought me a stack of cookbooks for little kids and told me I needed to learn how to cook. She said it would empower me. It was fun. I felt like a grown-up.

After much begging on my part she even bought me a puppy, so our new house was complete. I don't remember what kind of dog it was, just a regular rambunctious puppy. I was 8 years old and could make myself meals in my own kitchen, but I had no idea how to care for or train a small animal. The puppy peed on the floor and no amount of newspapers or rubbing of its nose trained it to stop. I didn't know how to raise a puppy right. I was failing. I was a bad mom. I was sitting on the stairs watching it pee on the floor again and the frustration overtook me. I could not speak. I could only clench my fists together and hold in a scream. My mom looked at me, concerned.

"What's the matter, honey? Tell me what you're feeling." I couldn't put it into words. I was just a stupid failure and couldn't take care of anything. "Honey, talk to me. Use your words." I couldn't talk. I hated her for telling me to speak about my feelings because I couldn't explain them. I didn't know how. I didn't know what to say.

I started smacking myself repeatedly on the face. My mother ran up the stairs to try to grab my hands to stop me, but I ran from her. I smacked myself as I ran. I was crying but it was relieving to hurt myself like that. It brought the pain forward onto my skin so I could feel it instead of keeping it in a place where I couldn't describe or understand it. My mom finally reached me and got hold of my hands, but I had already smacked myself enough. I had already felt the relief. She was really upset but she didn't know what to do. She kept asking me what was wrong but I just cried. From that point on, whenever I became overwhelmed with frustration or pain, I would hurt myself before anyone else could.

Day 7 of the search
Angela Shelton in the badlands of South Dakota

I've lost four Angela Sheltons so far. They changed their minds about my coming to see them. They don't want to tell their stories, hurt their perpetrators or families, or get too personal. I understand, but it's still annoying. I'm trying to look on the bright side that it saves me gas money. I call the third Angela Shelton in South Carolina again, the one who lives in my dad's town. She is the youngest Angela. She's 22. I'm half hoping that she'll back out too and I can avoid her city altogether.

"Hey there!" she says after I tell her who it is. She sounds excited.

"We're just coming up on the badlands in South Dakota. I'm on my way." I feel my stomach tighten. "I've been thinking about the fact that you live in my dad's town. I'm a little creeped out."

"Yeah, I know. I looked him up after we got off the phone the first time—you know, in the registry."

"You did?" This is getting too real too quickly.

"He wasn't on the offenders list." I'm relieved. He is my dad. "He never got caught, huh?"

"No, not really. I mean I heard he got caught at a few jobs way back when he was married to my mom, but they just fired him. There were never any charges. My mom told me that they had to move one time because he went over to somebody's house and took off all his clothes. Then he was a counselor at a boys' juvenile delinquent home and got busted doing something with the boys, but I don't have details. My grandfather told me a long time ago that my dad used to bring home one boy from the school and take him back to his room almost every afternoon and lock the door."

"Oh God," Angela sighs.

"Yeah, I know. But he was never officially caught."

"They rarely are. When was the last time you saw him?"

"Twelve years ago."

"Wow." I assume this Angela has a happy family.

"Well, that's not true. I saw him very briefly about two years ago. I was driving cross-country with my boyfriend, and we passed by where my dad was working. I had called him out of the blue right before we got there to confront him. He just cried and cried. He kept saying he didn't know what happened to us. I guess I felt sorry for him. I don't know how to explain it.

"When I was near him on that trip, I called him up and he met us at this little barbeque place. I didn't want to go to his house or anything. My boyfriend was so irritated that I wanted to see my dad. But we went. Then in the parking lot my dad told me he had something for me in his van."

"Eww," Angela gasps.

"Yeah, really. He opened the side door and grabbed a bag of Beanie Babies and handed it to me. Isn't that weird? His van was full of them."

"Oh my God."

"I know." I think back to the days when I was little and his van was filled with candy and toys. "He gave me some framed picture of him dangling a jelly worm in my mouth the last time I had seen him when I was 14 years old. Gross. Then he hugged me and ran his hand down my back and over my ass."

"He did not."

"He did. And it didn't even hit me until later when my boyfriend and I were back on the road for a few hours that my father had just rubbed my ass." I wish I could go back to that moment and give my father a piece of my mind or slap him across the face.

"Maybe we should drive by his house or something when you're here," Angela suggests.

"Oh yeah," I laugh uncomfortably. "Well, we still have a lot of Angela Sheltons to see before we get to you." I change the subject.

"I can't wait to meet you." Angela sounds more excited than I am. "I'm so interested to see how this all turns out. It's such a good idea."

I stare out the window and watch the mile signs move past. I wish that we could slow down. I'm not sure I agree this is a good idea anymore. I'm trying to fit all of these pieces together in my mind. I'm not even sure how this whole movie is going to come together. I feel like bursting into tears. I get off the phone and flip through my book of Angela Sheltons instead. I want to think about their lives in order to avoid my own.

1979

I ran away from my dad's house when I was 7 years old. Well, I tried to run away. I couldn't take living with my dad anymore. I hated him. I wanted my mom, and I was just going to leave and it would all be better. We were in a new house. My dad bought the A-frame on the lake. It was dark and looming. At that point my dad had cut off most of the contact I had with my mom. He let me see her a few times a year. On the rare occasions when I saw her, she said she didn't want to talk bad about my dad. She wanted to use the time to see me as much as possible. She told me she was trying to regain custody. My dad always said that my mother was nuts. He told me that she was a bad influence because she didn't go to church and she wore red nail polish and red lipstick. I thought he was the one who was crazy, and I wanted to get out of there. My dad was making us get naked all the time. We had to touch him too or he'd yell at us. I never told my mom. I was going to run away and find her instead.

I stuffed a pillowcase full of cans of food, a favorite pair of shorts, and some underwear. I was halfway down the dirt driveway when my stepbrother came after me.

"Where're you going?" he yelled, annoyed.

"I'm running away," I explained as I held onto my sack.

"Where're you going to go? You don't have anywhere to go." He had his hands on his hips. I looked at the ground. I'd find somewhere to go. Anywhere was better than where I was. Steve walked down the driveway and took a hold of my sack and peered into it.

"Angie, all you have in here are cans." He looked at me disgustedly, like I didn't know how to run away properly.

"Yeah, so?" I cocked my hip to one side like my dad showed my stepsister when he had all the porn magazines laid out. I knew how to lean my hips, and I knew that you were supposed to give canned goods at the school drive for kids in need. I was a kid in need, so I took cans when I ran away.

"You don't even have a can opener in here. How do you expect to get all of those cans open without a can opener?"

I stared at him. He had a point. I looked at the ground, defeated, and took my sack from him. I sure was stupid. Next time, I promised myself that I would at least get past the driveway and remember the damn can opener.

Day 8 of the search
Somewhere in Nebraska

I open a bottle of wine and wish I had a cigarette. I'm alone for the moment. Giovanni and Gallo share a room at night while the girls take the RV. Chantal and I share the RV bedroom, and Sylvia sleeps on the fold-out. We use the men's motel room to shower and watch TV before the men go to bed. Chantal and Sylvia are in there watching HBO right now. I have every intention of sharing the bottle with them when they come back, but I drink half of it before it's my turn to shower. My cell phone rings, pausing my exit. It's the alcoholic Angela again.

"Funny you should call me right now—I'm loaded too," I tell her. She laughs and slurps her beer.

"Why are you doing this?"

"Getting drunk?"

"No, doing this movie."

"Haven't you asked me that like 100 times already, Angela?" She just cackles and doesn't answer me. "I'm glad I amuse you so much." I wonder if I know the answer to her question. I pause, sip, and then pause again. "You could say I had a vision. I dreamed about this movie. I knew that it was going to inspire many people and change lives. I made a joke in a production meeting about searching for Angela Sheltons, but then afterward I had this dream about crowds of women celebrating. They were filling the streets like a big rally or something. I knew when I woke up that I had to make this move, that somehow it would help women in huge ways." I figure it doesn't matter if she thinks I'm crazy or not. She doesn't say anything, just laughs nervously and falls silent.

"I can't be in anything you're talking about. I'm not a good person."

"Angela, you're always saying that, and it's ridiculous."

"Yeah, but Angie, you're so pretty," she says, and I wonder what being pretty has to do with anything. "I'm nothing like you. I'm not pretty. I'm not a good person."

"You've never even met me. How do you know if I'm pretty or not?"

"Everyone is pretty compared to me."

"You can't compare yourself to anyone, Angela. We all have something to offer the world; otherwise we wouldn't be here." I swallow another half glass and look in the mirror in the tiny bathroom of the RV. I wonder if I'm pretty and what I have to offer the world. I spent 12 years being paid as a fashion model and being torn down for every single flaw I had. I'm not sure I even like myself, to be honest, but I don't share that. I wonder what this alcoholic Angela Shelton looks like. "We all have a story, Angela. You want to know what's funny?"

"What?" she half snorts like she could use a good joke.

"My father lives in Charleston, South Carolina." She starts laughing even though that's not the funny part. "And there are three Angela Sheltons in South Carolina. One of them lives in Charleston." Silence. "The Angela Shelton that lives in my dad's town is tracking sexual predators."

I hear Angela's refrigerator door open and close. I suspect she's getting another beer. I wait. "You freak me out." I feel like telling her that it freaks me out too, but I play it cool instead.

"Pretty wild, huh? Things are connected in the weirdest ways. That's why I can't wait to meet you too. All of the Angelas are filling in a giant puzzle, as if we're speaking for all women."

"You're never going to meet me because I'm nobody. I'm nothing."

"Ah, but, Angela, that is so untrue. You're an Angela Shelton. And you know what? You and I are much more alike than you even realize. We're both doing the same thing—we just have different ways of doing it." I don't get a response. I only hear a dial tone.

1980

My stepsister and I didn't know what to think about all these sudden changes. We sat in the social worker's truck, stunned. We were being driven to our new temporary home. The social workers called it a foster home. I was 8 and Lisa was 10. We had lived together for five years with her mom and my dad. We held hands in the back of the truck. I was worried about what my dad would do to us when he found out that we told. I think Lisa was worried too. I was sure my dad would go through his whole belt rack and beat us with each one as soon as he heard.

"This is only temporary," Ms. Lemons reminded us as she drove. "You two are only going to be in this home during the hearing while we determine the safest place for you to live."

"Will I go live with my dad?" Lisa asked. I had a moment of panic, thinking that was exactly what would happen. I wouldn't get to live with her anymore at all. Then I thought of my mom and had a moment of excitement.

"Will I get to go live with my real mom?"

"The judge has to decide all that. But you'll be safe from your dad while that's being decided," she said and then corrected herself, "Angie's dad." I looked at Lisa. I was so sorry. I was sorry that it was my dad who hurt her.

We pulled up to a plain house with a dirty screen door. A big woman in a muumuu stepped out onto the concrete porch. That was our new foster mother. Her skinny husband stepped out from behind her and underneath them came a 5-year-old boy. The boy peered at Lisa and me as we got out of the truck. His hands were sticky from too much candy. He was sticking them together and wiping them on the hem of his mom's muumuu. I could tell by the look he gave me that he didn't like us. I didn't understand why we had to be there. I wanted to go straight to my mom's house.

"This is only temporary. It's going to be OK," Ms. Lemons repeated as she walked us toward our new foster parents. Their son snarled at us as we reached the steps. His mother looked at us the same way. I wondered if she knew our story. I wondered if she thought we were dirty. I held onto Lisa's hand. It was my fault we were there, so I vowed to look out for her even though she was my big sister.

Dream Journal—May 10, 2001
I dreamed about riding the tricycle again. I was an adult this time. I was trying to work the pedals with my long legs while tugging the giant motor home behind me. I kept wondering what people were going to say if they came upon me trying to tug that huge thing down the road.

Day 9 of the search
Angela Shelton in Kansas

"This is just so neat," the Angela Shelton in Kansas says. She's Caucasian, is round with curly hair, and has a joyful glow about her. She and I giggle about how weird all of this is as my crew sets up. I follow her cat with my eyes around her bedroom. Angela strokes his head as she sits on the quilt that covers her bed. It makes me think of my grandmother. It makes me think of generations of women and patterns within families.

"What would you say is your purpose in life?" I ask Angela once the camera is aimed at her.

"Well, I'm here to serve the Lord. I want to help others."

"What would you say to women in America? Here is your chance."

Angela looks up at the ceiling, thinking, and then says, "I'd say, 'Don't be afraid to stand up for yourself and be yourself.'" I wonder if her comment is meant for me.

"Are you happy with where you're at?" I wonder what my answer would be to the same question. I'm not sure if I'm happy or not. I'm particularly good at appearing happy though. Angela seems happier than me. Here I am on the road asking other women how they live, like I'm seeing how other women cope with life.

"I'm very happy with where I'm at," Angela says. "Looking back it's been a pretty fulfilling life. There are a lot of things that I wanted to do and wanted to accomplish, and I have. And I'm only 31. There's still a lot out there to do." I smile at her, thinking about my answer to the same question. There is a lot that I want to do too, but then again, I guess I'm doing it. I'm happy that I'm interviewing one of my namesakes. I'm happy that I took a leap of faith and left on this road trip.

"I love the fact that you're a schoolteacher. What do you teach?"

"I teach middle school band, usually a wild bunch. It's sort of controlled chaos most of the time."

"Are there things you would change about the school system?"

"Besides paying teachers more? I think it all goes back to parenting. We need good parents. If kids are supported and loved, then they will be the best they can be. Then they become good parents. But it all starts with parenting. We should really have classes on parenting."

"Otherwise don't have kids, right?" I imagine parenting classes with brochures on not molesting or beating your children. There could be assignments on how to show healthy affection. "What do you love most about the world?"

"God, my family, and my friends—in that order."

"And you put God first?" I wonder if that might be the secret behind her glow.

"You have to put God first. I've been spending a lot of time thinking about the big picture, how I should live my life, and what God has planned for me. And God has given me a sense of hope and a direction in my life. I'm working on sharing that hope with others."

I wonder what God has planned for me as I stare at this Angela Shelton. "What do you think about the fact that so many of the Angela Sheltons I've spoken to have been raped, beaten, or molested?" Angela is quiet for a moment. She strokes her cat. I watch her hand and wonder if she has a past of abuse as well.

"I guess I'm glad that nothing like that ever happened to me. But I'd like to give hope to the people who are hopeless, that need something more." I think about the alcoholic Angela and wonder what number beer she's on.

"There's an Angela Shelton that isn't doing too well. She could use some hope." I think maybe I'm talking about myself and not the alcoholic. Angela looks concerned and waits to hear more. "She thinks she's lower than a dog."

Angela sighs, taking in a deep breath like she can understand. "I'll pray for her. I'll pray that she finds hope and peace." Angela grins, looking like a sage sitting there on her quilt-covered bed. I wish all these Angelas could meet each other. I fiddle with the peace-of-heart pin in my hair.

On our way out of Kansas I wonder what life would be like if I took a page from the Angela Shelton guide for living and put God first. I wonder if that's possible or just another layer of denial. I think about my family and the hypocrisy of going to church on Sunday and beating kids on Monday. We drive past a billboard advertising crayons. Crayons were a favorite tool of my father's. He used crayons and markers as abuse tools on my stepsister. She told me about it years later. I'm annoyed that I'm reminded of my dad every day. I shake the image of him from my mind and try to think more about God as we merge onto the highway.

1977

My father left his mark on the side of every road he ever drove. He was a litterbug. "Roll down the winder," he would tell my stepmother when we were on our way to yet another nudist colony. My stepmother always did what my father told her to do. She never questioned him. It was like she was in a trance. She rolled down her window, and he tossed our family-size McDonald's white paper bag past her, out her window, and onto the side of the highway. I watched from the back of the station wagon where I sat across from my stepsister as the bag hit the ground and burst open, revealing our cups and napkins and Styrofoam burger containers. The bag became smaller and smaller as we drove farther and farther away. I peered over the backseat at my dad and vowed never to litter as he nonchalantly continued driving and my stepmother rolled her window back up. I thought my dad was an ass and didn't care about anything in the world but himself.

"Time to take your clothes off," he ordered. He was grinning. We must have been getting close to the latest nudist camp. Those camps were his favorite vacation spots. My dad always got excited when we went to any of his nudist colonies. He liked to be naked, and he liked us to be naked too. We had to do as he said. It was better than getting beaten. If any of us ever complained, we got his belt on our bare butts. My dad had a whole rack of them hanging on the door of his closet for the purpose of whipping. He was wearing one, so my stepbrother, stepsister, and I followed his orders and began scooting out of our britches.

"And you too." My dad glanced at my stepmother and gave her a wink. He reached over into her lap as she slid out of her pants. I knew what he was doing. He had already shown us how he put his fingers inside her. We'd already watched him put his big thing inside of her too. He said it was sex education in the home. I could see him from the back of the station wagon pulling his big thing out of his zipper. I wondered if the men in the passing cars were doing the same thing.

Day 10 of the search
Angela Shelton somewhere in America

The alcoholic Angela is hiding from me. We drive to where she works, and Gallo films it discreetly as if we're doing investigative reporting. I walk down the hall with my stomach in a knot. I have no idea how she's going to react to me just showing up. I get to the office I've been pointed toward and gently open the door. I'm greeted by a few smiling faces as women walk back and forth from their cubicles. The reception desk is empty, so I wait. A smiling lady comes toward me after a moment.

"Can I help you?"

"I'm looking for Angela Shelton."

"Oh, she's not in today. She went home." We stare at each other for a moment. She looks curious.

"I'm Angela Shelton. I'm the Angela Shelton searching for other Angela Sheltons." A few chairs roll out from their cubicles to have a peak at me.

"Oh, great. Angela told us about that. That is so cool."

"She did?" I remember Angela telling me how her coworkers had said this idea was so stupid. They didn't look like they thought it was stupid. "Do you know if she still lives here?" I flip to Angela's page in my binder. I have an address for her from my first Internet search. The lady leans over and reads the address I point to.

"Oh, she's moved since then, but she's not too far from there. We're not supposed to give that information out, but since it's you, I guess we can make an exception." She smiles and reaches for a notepad. "So you're interviewing all the Angela Sheltons in the country?"

"Yes, I'm not even halfway through yet. I've kind of just started."

"Are they all pretty neat?" Another coworker steps up beside her and grins at me. I smile back.

"Our Angela Shelton is a pretty neat lady."

"What made you pick the name Angela Shelton?"

"It's my name. It's just a way to survey women in America."

"Too bad you didn't pick my name," one lady huffs. "I want to be in a movie." I watch her head back to her cubicle.

"Here's her address. You'll know her car by the Beanie Babies in the back. It's lined with them." I think about my dad and his van full of them. I take the address from her, thank her, and head back down the hallway toward the exit.

We follow the directions to Angela's new apartment. I pull the big RV across the street from her window. We all peer through the blinds of the mini kitchen window in the RV. I figure Angela is doing the same right back at us. The crew is nervous. They've heard all the stories of the late night phone calls and been privy to some of them.

Giovanni clips a microphone to my collar. I climb down the steps and make my way to Angela's house while the crew stays in the motor home and records me. I don't want to walk up to Angela's door with a group of people, a camera, and a boom aimed at her. I can see her move behind her shades as I approach her door.

"Angela," I call out in my Southern accent. "I told you I was going to come see you." I can hear her laughing on the other side of the door. "Come out, come out, wherever you are."

The door opens a crack and the alcoholic Angela Shelton leans out like a little girl playing hide-and-seek. She is much shorter than me and blonde with an adorable smile. "Hello," she says meekly. I remember all the times she said that she was lower than a dog and how she's not pretty. I am amazed to see such an adorable girl trapped inside a grown woman's body standing before me. Her low opinion of herself shines in her eyes without her uttering a word.

"May I come in?"

"Um. Well, I forgot that I have to meet someone, and she's not here yet but she will be here any minute," she assures me. "And then I can meet with you after she gets here." I wonder for a second if she's talking about her drunken self.

"Well, do you want us to come back then? I told you I was going to come here." I smile at her.

"I see that." She smiles back.

"I'll tell you what. It's not like you don't have my number. Call me when you're ready, after your friend shows up." I step away from her door. She starts to laugh.

"Of course I have your number." She must have it committed to memory at this point. She looks at me sideways. "Oh, and you better bring beer. Busch beer," she says, sort of gasps, and then shuts the door in my face. I stand there for a second before walking back across the street to the RV. My crew stares at me expectantly, all except Giovanni, who heard the whole thing in his earphones.

"So you think she's going to call you?" he asks.

"Yeah, she'll call. She called me almost every night in LA, drunk. I've spoken to her more than any other Angela. She'll call."

We find a motel down the street, and in honor of Angela Shelton, we all pop open some beers and sit and chill out while we wait for her "friend" to arrive. It takes about two hours but she finally calls my cell phone. She is lit.

"There was no friend," she admits as if I should have figured that out by now. "I couldn't talk to you unless I was drunk."

"I thought your friend might be your beer," I say, and she howls with laughter. I wonder if I'm dealing with a wacko or a wounded girl. I figure there's a little bit of both.

"Bring more beer," she orders. I don't think getting her beer is such a good idea, so I buy Coronas instead of her favorite beer and drive back to her house. I park across the street like I did earlier. Giovanni puts the microphone on me again. I grab the six-pack and head back toward her door. Her windows are lit with the glow of lamplight as I approach and knock. She opens the door on wobbly legs. She's grinning.

"Where's your crew?" Her eyes dart around me.

"They're in the RV waiting. I didn't want to barge in here with the camera going. You told me you didn't want to be on film," I remind her.

"I'm ugly," she says and nods. I roll my eyes.

"You are not ugly, Angela. I'm so sick of hearing you say that." She stares at me and then quickly motions me inside. "I brought you beer like you said." I lift up the six-pack. She looks excited and then snubs her nose.

"I don't drink that. I only drink one kind. And you just brought beer to an alcoholic."

"I know. I didn't know whether I should or not. At least it's a kind you don't like. I just want to talk to you." I feel like an ass. "What a cute place you have." I change the subject.

"Look at my angel." She pulls me into her bedroom like she's a little girl showing me her room. She points to a picture of an angel on the wall. She is very proud as she motions to it.

"Is that you?" I ask. She scoffs like that is the most ridiculous thing imaginable.

"No." She looks me up and down. "This is weird," she mumbles. I nod, thinking the same thing. She heads out of the room and back into the kitchen. I follow her. She opens the re-frigerator, and I catch a glimpse of beer cans lined up for battle. She pulls one out, opens it, takes a swig, and then stares at me like we're meeting for the first time on a planet far away. A train whistles loudly in the distance. We stare at each other as it makes its way toward us. It seems like it's going right through her apartment. I don't remember seeing train tracks. I wonder if it's an imaginary train for a moment, urging her every day to get on board. We stand there, letting it pass and fade into the distance.

"I did write notes," she says suddenly like she just remembered them. She sways over to the coffee table and picks up a few sheets of violet-colored paper like a little girl would have. She looks at them for a second and then hands them to me.

"Can I read these?"

"Yes." She flips her hands toward the notes like I'm crazy not to read them. I look down at the girlie cursive writing. It looks like a 10-year-old wrote it. It's a list of numbered comments. I move to the sofa and she follows me.

"*I live such a lie,*" I read and look over at her as she sits down next to me. She looks like she wants to tell me something. I think of her "friend" coming over to visit as I stare at the empty cardboard case of beer on the floor.

"I do. I live such a lie. Everybody thinks I'm so great, and I'm not." She looks at me. I think of the girls at work telling me how neat she is. "OK, go to the next one." She points to the notes in my hand.

"*Alcoholism is a family tradition.*"

"It is. It's a family tradition."

"Did your father drink?"

"Oh, yes," she says as if there wasn't a day he didn't.

"Did your father ever beat your mother?" I ask point blank. Angela looks at me quickly and fiercely like I just read her diary. "I was just curious." Angela sits there staring at the tissue box by the sofa.

"My mother was a good woman. I never told you how she was abused."

"No, but there are patterns in families. It's not that hard to figure out. Did he hit her?" Tears begin to flow down Angela's cheeks. I've hit a nerve.

"Oh yeah." She sails off into a memory. She speaks as if she's a little girl again. "I would try and stop it, but I couldn't. He pushed her down one time, and I tried to hit him, but he shoved me. My mom was on the floor . . ." She stops for a moment and just sits there and cries. She wipes her face quickly as if she's afraid of getting in trouble. I can relate. "And I was just lower than a dog," she whispers. "Lower than a dog . . . Oh, my sister . . . My sister died," she sighs, moving to another memory.

"Was she an alcoholic too?"

"Oh, yes." She waves at me like that was a stupid question. "It's a family tradition, remember? Go to the next one." She points to the papers in my hand as if she just snapped back to reality and remembered where she left off. I look down at the papers and keep reading.

"*You've caught me at a very low time in my life. I feel like I'm a failure. I hate living this lie, but I do a good job at it,*" I read. Angela nods and I continue, "*I love comedians, I love humor, I love to laugh. My acting debut.*" I look at the paper and then at her. We smile at each other. I go to the next item on the list. "*It's a godsend.* What's a godsend?"

"You."

"That's nice." I don't know what else to say. I don't feel like much of a godsend.

"No really, Angela," she says and then looks at me like she just figured out that we share a name. "You're Angela! Angela Shelton. Hello!"

"You're Angela too. We are all Angela."

"I'm ugly," she whispers quickly and quietly.

"Oh, Angela. You've got to stop with that. I don't think you're ugly at all." She's really adorable actually, but no amount of my saying that is going to get through to her.

"Yes, I am. I'm ugly."

"You know what? That's like your father saying to you that—"

"That I am lower than a dog," she finishes my sentence for me.

"You're lower than a dog. Right. That's nice." I'm amazed that a parent could say such a thing to a child. I'm amazed that people are allowed to procreate and then treat their offspring like animals.

"But I am," Angela announces like I'm crazy to doubt it.

"So you believe him?" I strike another chord. Angela falls into a heap of tears on the couch beside me. "Oh, sweetie . . ." I rub her arm. "Can I give you a hug?" I reach over to hug her before she has a chance to say no. We sit like that for a minute before she leans back and wipes her tears.

"Where's your crew?" she asks like a little girl.

"They're in the RV. Do you want to meet them?"

"Yes," she says confidently. She downs the rest of her beer, goes to the refrigerator, grabs another one, and heads for the door on a full lean. She looks at me as if to tell me to get the hell up and take her to my ship on wheels. I follow her out her door and across the street. I knock on the door of the RV, and Gallo pulls it open. I tell him not to turn the camera on.

"They don't have the camera, do they?" Angela asks just as Gallo slides it back into the bag.

"No, you're fine." She follows me inside like a nervous puppy.

We all stare at each other. Angela is so wasted that I'm sure she won't remember any of this. Giovanni gets up and moves to another seat and gives her a place at the table. She sits down. "This is so cool," she mumbles as she looks around the RV. We try to make small talk with her, but Angela starts crying within moments of sitting down. She's very drunk. She starts mumbling things about her dad and how she's lower than a dog and will never be as cool as any of us. I sit next to her at the kitchenette table and tell her that none of that is true, that she is special. She just shakes her head from side to side and after a while just gets up and falls toward the RV door. I let her grab onto me and walk her back to her door. We hug uncomfortably.

"I hope you get help, Angela."

"I need it," she mumbles quietly and then looks at the ground. I grab the bag of beer that I brought, which is still sitting on the floor by the door. At least I'll take away my own mistake, but there's nothing I can do about the cases of beer still left.

"Call me."

"Oh, I will. You're on my drunk dial list," she laughs and cries in the same breath and then slams the door in my face.

1978

I was 6 when I learned how to swim. My father tossed me into the pool on one of our family vacations. He picked me up and tossed me right in and told me to make it to the other side. I had no other choice but to do as he said or I was going to drown. I didn't want to die, so I swam like I had seen my stepbrother and stepsister swim. I made it to the other side. I didn't die. I followed my father's orders and I learned how to swim out of necessity. I saved my own life instead of dying on vacation. At least we were at a normal motel and not a nudist camp. At least I didn't die naked and killed by my own father tossing me into the deep end of the pool.

I held on to the edge, panting and nervous. I looked back at my dad on the other side of the pool. He was cheering and laughing. I thought he was a jerk and almost told him so, but I didn't feel like getting a whipping. I was on the other side of the pool. I had made it. I had swum the whole way. I didn't know whether to hate my dad or thank him.

Dream Journal—May 10, 2001
    I dreamed about the dollhouse that my father gave me when I was eleven. He wasn't supposed to see me after the court hearing but he dropped it off at my mom's house anyway. It had electricity and little lights in each room. I dreamed I was turning on all the lights but couldn't get any of them to work.

Day 11 of the search
Angela Shelton in Missouri

"I thought you were crazy," the Angela Shelton in Missouri admits. She's a stout, pretty, Caucasian brunette who is cheery despite the flood warnings. It hasn't stopped raining since we left California. It has rained, poured, or drizzled at least once every day of this trip. The Missouri Angela and her two daughters just returned from the swimming pool. The rain didn't stop a swim in this heat. A Jack Daniel's cooler sits on the coffee table. It makes me think of the alcoholic Angela. I wonder if she's at work with a hangover right now. I wonder if she even gets hangovers anymore. The Missouri Angela adjusts her swimming suit under her damp T-shirt. "I figured you didn't have anything better to do with your time, to be honest. But when you called me from Montana and said you were on your way, I was like, oh my God, she is really coming here. I wondered if you were a lunatic, but then my friend looked you up on the Internet and found *Tumbleweeds* and a bunch of other things about you, and I was like, yep, that's her. You seemed all right when we talked on the phone, not too crazy." She laughs. "And this seems like a neat idea. What are your questions? Do you have a list of them?"

"Just broad questions like who are you, where have you been, and where are you going? And what would you say to other women, like words of wisdom, helpful hints, or advice?"

Angela Shelton tilts her head to one side, thinking. "What would I say to women? First of all I'd tell them that they don't have to be married to be themselves, and no man anywhere can make them into themselves. You are you."

Angela seems so strong and tough. I stare at her, not knowing what to say. It seems that the Angela Sheltons have it all figured out much more than I do. I figure that it's just me and the alcoholic Angela who have issues. I feel like going into a diatribe about all my past relationships and how I've been with unavailable, angry men or men I supported like my mom supported my dad, but I remain silent. I figure that's an entirely different movie. I want to tell this Angela that I've been married twice already just because they asked and my self-esteem was the size of a peanut. I don't even count that I've been married really. I don't even feel like I was present, awake, or aware. It was as if I married them to play some part and it wasn't me. I've always been with a man who liked me or wanted me just because he did. That's probably directly related to my dad never wanting me, but

I don't want to talk about him. Then Angela Shelton might really think I'm crazy.

"That's great advice. I need to take it," I say instead.

"Most of us do."

"But you're married now, right?"

"Yes, for the third time, and he's wonderful. He really is. It's like a honeymoon all the time with that man, but like I said, he doesn't make me into me. I can't stand all that 'you complete me' crap because that idea is totally off. That's what I would say to women: Don't put all your faith in a man saving you. No one can save you but yourself, and that's it." I wish I had a big gong to hit on that point. I need to tattoo that on my own forehead so that I see it every day in the mirror.

Angela's phone rings and goes straight to the machine. We all pause while it clicks on. It's her husband. "Hey, honey, I'm just calling to say I love you. Call me when you can." Then it beeps. I smile at Angela.

"Perfect timing."

"He's pretty great. But like I said, you have to find yourself on your own; otherwise no man will ever fit into your life. You'll always be trying to make him into something he's not or make yourself into something to fit what he wants. That will never work." Angela stares at me. I wonder if I have a neon sign of low self-esteem on my face. "We all have our issues. Mine is stress. I thrive on it. I'm always doing something. I can't sit still. I always have something to take care of or fix. I do that so I'll have something to do. Just to sit does not work for me. The same things goes with my hair. I can never just leave it alone. I'm always changing my hairstyle." We both laugh. Her hair is certainly coiffed at the moment. "You gotta do something in a small town like this; otherwise you'll go crazy. People think we're nuts, but really they are. I do crazy things and get talked about all the time. For instance, I put fake flowers in my front yard. Did you see them? I love doing that."

"That's awesome. I'll have to check them out."

"People will find all kinds of reasons to talk about you," Angela continues. "I bet they'll go on about this movie too. They talk and talk like they don't have anything better to do when really it keeps them from looking at themselves. That's the truth of it. My husband and I drive 80 miles outside of town to go dancing so we don't stir up the whole town here."

"Really? That's awesome. Why so far away?"

"We drive over to the black area. They know how to dance, and it's more fun and more open, and we love it. There are so many bigots around here it would make you crazy."

"I know, I grew up in the South. And I've always wished that I was a black woman."

"I hear that." Angela leans her head back and laughs.

"Because they're so strong, and they'll kick your butt. I know not every one—that's a generalization—but I went to an all-black school once when I was younger and I always loved those black women. I wanted to be one. They didn't take lip from anybody."

"So just be one," Angela suggests. "Stop taking lip and stand up for yourself. Find that inner black woman." She laughs again. "That's why I go dancing—to realize my inner strength." She tosses her head back. I love her.

"I need to dance," I admit. "It's one of my all-time favorite things to do, and I've been with so many men who tell me to pipe down, behave, sit down, calm down. I'm kind of a wild dancer, that's why."

"But that goes right back to how no man can tell you how to be you," Angela coaches me.

"You're right. I should just dance. I wish we were staying longer. I'd go with you and your husband."

"We'd love to have you. Looking at you, I wouldn't think you'd have issues like that. You're a fancy Hollywood celebrity." I laugh out loud.

"We all have our issues though, right?" I don't feel like diving all the way into mine at the moment, so I ask Angela about her childhood instead.

"My parents were wonderful as far as parents go. They provided me with everything. I couldn't want for anything. I grew up in a beautiful home, but I was very sheltered, as if life were perfect and the world were wonderful. That's what I grew up thinking. And it's not. It's not even close."

"What do you mean?"

"Well, take this town for instance. You drove through it. Almost every other house is a meth lab in this town."

"No, really? I never would've thought that."

"No, you wouldn't, and that's the problem. People can't believe it's happening, so it happens right under their noses."

"Wow. That's just like the secret of child sexual abuse. It can be right under your nose and still be ignored or not believed."

"That's exactly right. That's exactly why I watch my kids. I let them know what's going on and what to be aware of because they need to know. It's like you with the story you told me about your dad. People need to understand. We need to teach our children how to protect themselves, and we need to protect them better."

"It's true. My dad was a perfectly nice guy who no one would suspect was acting like he did behind closed doors."

"See. And you probably lived right next door to a meth lab."

"And the neighbors are too busy making fun of your fake flowers to notice what's going on."

"Right?" She giggles. "It is going to be a very interesting world when people begin to wake up and smell the coffee about what's going on around them."

"Seems like we need to get rid of all the meaningless judgment we place on each other first. That seems like it's one of the things that's busy blinding us."

"That's right. We need to do our hair however we want to, dance whenever we want to, and put fake flowers wherever we want to too. And we need to wake up and look around and open our eyes. We're paying attention to the wrong things," Angela Shelton declares.

1977

My dad moved us all into a new house that had a white picket fence. It was perfect. That was when he was still promising my mom that she could see me anytime. But I didn't get to see her very much. My dad came up with lots of reasons. He told me my mother was not leading a good life. He told me I had the good family and was better off not seeing my mom so much. He said she would be a bad influence on me. He didn't want me telling her about the things we did either. He told us all that what we did behind closed doors was what all families did. We were perfect, but we shouldn't talk about it. We should just do as we were told like everyone else.

We had to massage my dad and his new wife. They would lie out on the waterbed, and Lisa and I had to massage my dad while Steve had to massage his mom. They were both naked. My dad instructed us where to put our hands. His big thing stood at attention between his legs. He told my sister and me how to rub it up and down. He had us squirt lotion all over him and rub him. He made us get naked too. It was strange. I wanted to say how weird it was, but I didn't. I wondered if other families really did the same thing.

"This is what everyone does," my dad assured us. "We don't talk about what everyone does because everyone is doing it."

I wasn't supposed to tell anybody about our family vacations to the nudist colonies either. My dad coached us before we went to each new one. He made us stand naked in a big circle and look at each other's bodies. "Guys are only going to like you if you're pretty," he told my stepsister. "Cock your hip to one side like they do in the magazines." He pulled out some of his porno magazines and showed us how the naked ladies posed correctly. My stepmother didn't do anything to stop him so I figured it was OK. I tried to do the same pose that my dad moved my stepsister into. "Now we just need to get your teeth fixed. No boy is going to like you with those crooked teeth."

I ran to the bathroom and smiled into the mirror. I had crooked teeth too. I figured that no boy was ever going to like me either. I cocked my hip to one side like my dad showed my stepsister, but I couldn't get it right. I wasn't sexy like my dad liked. I was an ugly girl with crooked teeth.

Day 12 of the search
Angela Shelton still in Missouri

"I'm worried about something," the Missouri Angela Shelton says quietly. "I told you some things yesterday that I don't think should be out there in the world." She looks nervous and upset.

She has the signed release in her hand and keeps looking down at it as she speaks. A nervous neighbor lurks on the sidewalk.

"OK. I won't use whatever you don't want me to," I assure her, trying to make her feel at ease.

"The neighbors are all worried about the fact that ya'll are from Hollywood."

I laugh, figuring they have something new to focus on besides her fake flowers. "I can assure you that I won't use anything you don't want me to. This is about inspiring women, not upsetting them. What do you not want me to use?" Angela goes down a list of things. To make her feel better, I even write out a paragraph on the release about what I will not include in the film. I initial it and do the same on her copy. I don't know whether it's official or not, but it makes us both feel better. I have no intention of using any part of an Angela's story that she doesn't want me to use. I even scratch out some of what she told me from my journal.

After I deal with the legal matters, the nosy neighbor slowly makes his way farther and farther down the street, keeping one eye cocked toward me the entire time. I walk past Angela's flowerbed and grin. I get into my Hollywood rented RV and drive out of town on my way to meet another Angela Shelton. Some neighbors peek suspiciously at me and my crew through their blinds, and I wonder if they're hiding meth labs.

1976

My father was a liar. He always acted charming and funny when we were in public. He made everyone laugh. He hugged me and sat me on his lap and told stories. He made lots of jokes when we had company over. I always wondered what would happen if those people saw the other side of my dad, the angry side. My dad was a great actor. If we lived someplace else I figured my dad would have been on TV or in the movies instead of selling candy.

My dad would send us to bed without dinner if we let on that everything was not as peachy as it seemed to company. We would get a glass of Tang or instant iced tea and a slice of tangerine. I would sit in my room hungry and pretend that I was trapped in a dungeon where an evil monster was hoarding all the food. I declared that I would find a way out of there one day. I would become as good an actor as my dad. I would weasel my way into the dark side and pretend to be one of them. I would find food and water and help all the prisoners escape.

Day 13 of the search
Angela Shelton in Illinois

"It makes me feel like I'm not alone," Angela Shelton in Illinois says when we arrive at the hospital at which she works. She's a pretty Caucasian nurse with dirty blonde hair and a jolly demeanor. "It makes me feel like I'm not the abnormal one," she says after I tell her about all the Angelas. "It's like everybody else got the *Brady Bunch* family and I had a different family. So this makes me feel like I'm not alone. I love that you're making this movie."

"What would you like to tell other women?"

"Um, that you don't have to be suppressed. That you can be an independent woman and not rely on a man." Again Angela Shelton is talking directly to me.

"Do you like yourself?" I figure that might be the secret to independence.

"I do. I have rough days though."

"Angela is the best nurse there is," Angela's nursing partner shouts from the other side of the room. "I don't know what I'd do without Miss Angela Shelton."

"Other people like you too." We both grin back at the nurse.

"I love Angela Shelton. I just love what ya'll are doing too. I wish my name was Angela Shelton." Giovanni has to change a sound tape, so I walk with Angela over to her fellow nurse. Kelly's a cute blonde who's full of giggles and grins. "Do you think this is going to be on TV? I mean that would be so cool."

"I don't know. I hope so."

"That would be so great. What made you want to do this?"

"I wanted to survey women in America. And I want to make a movie that inspires women, something that shows us that we really are awesome and we really are getting there." The two nurses nod. "I knew I would tell my story at some point during the making of this movie, but I haven't done that yet. I haven't had the time to go into it because as soon as I mention that I was abused, I find out that so many other people have been abused also. Most of the Angela Sheltons were raped, beaten, or molested. It's sad and eye-opening." Angela shakes her head in disgust and pain. Kelly mimics her.

"So how were you abused?" Kelly asks quietly.

"I was molested."

"I was too," Kelly discloses quietly. Angela sticks her hands in her pockets and looks at the floor. I can only assume from the look on her face that she's heard this story before and it makes her sad.

"I'm sorry. It's amazing how practically everyone I meet knows someone who was sexually abused. It's like a nightmare."

"It is. It really is," Angela says. "A nightmare."

"The problem is that no one is talking about it," Kelly says. "We never told. That's why it's so good that you guys are out talking about it."

"It's just sort of happening like that. I start to share my story and all of a sudden the floodgates open."

Angela looks at the floor again. I look over at her. She already told me on the phone that her sister was raped. I want to talk to her about it, but I don't want to go into it here in the hospital. Angela still has to finish her shift, so we pack up the camera gear, hug her and Kelly, and drive around Illinois until Angela gets off work.

We arrive at her lovely home in the middle of suburbia just after 5 p.m. Her manicured lawn and painted shutters do not look abnormal like the life she described having. I think about the Angela in Missouri telling us about all the meth labs behind the pretty front doors. Angela comes out wearing a bright yellow shirt and sits on a perfectly quilted quilt on a perfect lawn with a perfect breeze on a perfect May afternoon. She giggles, making the whole picture even more surreal.

"It looks like you have a perfect life."

Angela laughs and nods. "It's great now, but it wasn't always great, that's for sure. Growing up was hard."

"How come?"

"Well, my parents married really young, I mean really young. I think my mom was just 16. And they moved into my grandparents' house, and my grandfather was physically and verbally abusive to my grandmother, and that was hard to watch. Plus my mother has a mental illness. It started when she was pretty young, but as she grew older, the mental illness became worse."

"What kind of disorder?"

"Oh, everything. Paranoid schizophrenia. She hallucinated. She heard voices in her head. It was real bad, and like I said, it just got worse."

"What do you think caused her illness? Or did she always have it?"

"Well, when my mother was growing up, she was molested by her father." My mouth drops open. Angela never mentioned that on the phone.

"What happened? Did he ever get caught?"

"No. There's a lot of history of abuse in our family." I think of all the women throughout history who were carted off to insane asylums, drugged, or even lobotomized when they were labeled "crazy" or "hysterical." I wonder if they were suffering from incest survivor's syndrome and no one knew it was an epidemic, let alone how to treat it. I wonder if Angela's mother had been able to tell her story, if that would have made a difference in her mental health. "Then my parents got their own place next door to my grandparents, so my grandparents lived right next door to us. They helped out a lot to make sure my and my sister's needs were met when my mom was sick."

"And your grandfather was the one who was abusive?"

"Oh yeah, he was very abusive to my grandmother."

"Did anything ever happen with any of you kids?"

"No, that was my other grandfather. My grandmother remarried the year I was born, so I never even met my first grandfather."

"So that's a different grandfather than the one who was violent?"

"Yes." We both laugh. It's hard to keep track of all the limbs of family trees sometimes.

"From a child molester to a wife beater," I say.

"And if you look at the list of child molesters, my grandfather is also on that one."

I stop laughing, but she doesn't. I feel like I'm going to vomit. I swallow hard and take a deep breath. "How so?"

"Well, the woman he left my grandmother for had a 13-year-old daughter. This is so embarrassing . . ." Angela pauses and resituates herself on her quilt. "A fellow shopper was pushing her shopping cart past his van, and my grandfather was in the van with the 13-year-old on his lap, fondling her, and the shopper turned him in."

"Good that he was turned in."

"Yeah."

"There's something about vans."

"Yes, there's something about vans."

"My dad drove a van and still does."

"Oh, does he?" Angela looks at me sideways, concerned. I already told her on the phone about my dad, so she knows some of my story. "Maybe it's because they have all that space in the back and it's enclosed and private so nobody can see what's going on in the back of the van." We sit there staring at each other, not knowing what to say next.

"That's a good point. It's amazing how many women will stay with abusive men in order to not be alone."

"I know." Angela shakes her head. "Low self-esteem, I guess. My grandmother didn't kick my grandfather out until he almost paralyzed her."

"Oh my God."

"He knocked her down the steps, and she fell and hit her back. For a moment she couldn't move and thought he'd paralyzed her. That's when she decided to leave him. It had to get that bad." Angela stares off into the distance. She is silent as birds chirp a cheery song above her head.

"My stepmother stayed with my dad until he tried to kill her too." We both half laugh at the similarities.

"Did she really?"

"Apparently my stepmother found out that my dad was cheating on her. It didn't bother her that he was molesting her kids, but he cheats on her and she decides to leave him. She was babysitting her friend's child. He was around 2 years old. She went into the bathroom after she told my father she was leaving him. My dad followed her into the bathroom with a machete and told her that he was going to kill her and then kill himself because he couldn't live without her. Nice, huh?" It seems like I'm talking about soap opera characters and not my own family.

"What happened?"

"For the first time in her life my stepmother got some brains, I guess, because she quickly told my dad that the child she was babysitting would find their dead bodies and that wouldn't be a good thing for a 2-year-old to see. And as soon as my dad calmed down a bit, she slipped by him, grabbed the kid, made a beeline for her car, and drove away."

"Good for her."

"Thank God. There are so many women in this world who protect abusers though. It makes me sick."

"I know. It's like they can't accept it, and they ignore it or live in a fog of denial so they're not alone. Sick. And your stepmother knew it was going on?"

"She would open the door and send us into the bedroom with my dad. Or be in there with him and have us do stuff to her too."

"My God, Angela." She moves her head from side to side like she's trying to erase that image from her mind like an Etch A Sketch. "Did he do anything to you?"

"Oh yeah. I had to go into the room with him, but when I went in there, I went in with my stepsister. I never had to go alone like she did. We'd have to go in there and jerk him off."

"Oh my God."

"But I get to go see him," I announce to change the mood. "I told you that there's an Angela Shelton in his town, right?"

"Yes, you did. Doesn't she do something with the law?"

"She tracks sexual predators." Angela smiles like the Cheshire cat. "She's going to school for criminal justice and to make money she is an undercover security guard. She catches sex offenders, child molesters, pickpockets, and general weirdos. She's writing her paper for school on pedophiles."

"Isn't that amazing?"

"I know, right? She's in his town too. I have to go see him, right?" I ask, trying to convince myself as well as her. Angela nods an affirmative.

"What are you going to say to him?"

"I have no idea." I haven't thought that far ahead. I try not to think about my dad or the Angela in his town.

"Are you going to confront him?"

"I did already in a letter, but he didn't respond. I wrote out this huge 10-page letter about two years ago. I was very detailed and angry, and I laid it all out. I couldn't believe that I actually mailed it."

"Do you think he read it?"

"I have no idea. All I know is that he never responded. And I think it's so funny and weird that there's an Angela Shelton in his town. Well, not funny in a funny way; but then again, I hide everything with humor." I know Angela understands because she seems to do the same thing.

"Sometimes that's what you have to do," she admits. "When you've been through some of the things that we have, you have to laugh at it sometimes in order to deal with it. Otherwise it's too sad."

"Hopefully this movie will help. If so many of the Angelas were abused, that says something about women in general, doesn't it?"

"Yes, it does. I like that you're doing this. We need to pay attention to what's going on."

"Didn't you tell me on the phone that your sister was raped?" I ask, not knowing how to get into that subject.

"Yeah," Angela says in a whisper and then looks at the ground. She fidgets with a piece of grass.

"Do you want to talk about it?" Angela is silent. The birds above her become quiet too. It's as if they know the story she's about to tell. I wait. Angela breaks a blade of grass in half, then looks up at me and nods her head.

"It was the worst night of my life. New Year's Eve. We'd gone to a party for a woman I work with and her husband. These were friends of ours—we trusted them. We'd been out with them before, and we knew them, and like I said, I worked with this woman. So I brought my sister with me to this party, and she was at the bar talking to some other friends of mine. It was a big party." Angela trails off into a memory. "My husband and I were talking to some other people. There were a lot of nurses there, and I remember looking over and seeing that my sister and this other girl had fallen asleep by the Christmas tree. We went on about the party, drinking and carrying on, and I looked over at my sister again and she was gone. I started looking through the house for her and couldn't find her. Then I went and got my husband to start looking with me. I heard her in one of the rooms in the hallway. I tried to open the door, but it was locked."

"Oh my God."

"Yeah, this man, the husband of the woman I worked with, had carried my sister into his daughter's bedroom and had his way with her." The anger on her face is fresh, as if it just happened.

"How did you find that out?"

"I went and grabbed another friend of mine. He was a male nurse and a big guy. He came with me and was banging on the door and finally shoved it open and broke the lock. My sister was laying there on the floor crying."

"Where was the woman's husband?"

"He was standing right there, the bastard."

"No."

"Yes. He just looked at us like nothing was wrong and walked right past us back to the party." I shake my head like she did when I was telling her about my dad. "But I only cared about my sister right then. I ran into the room and sat beside her and she was mentally coming in and out. She'd had a lot to drink, I will say that."

"That's still no excuse. But they sure can hold that against her in court."

"I know," Angela says from experience. "Her stockings and panties were missing; she was crying. It was awful. I went nuts."

"What did you do?"

"I started going off on my friend's husband. I was yelling and screaming. Then my husband and his friends all started scouring that house for my sister's stockings and underwear. We never found anything, but they lived in a huge house on lots of acres. There's no telling where he hid them."

"Crap."

"I know."

"What was the guy's wife doing?"

"Oh, she was going nuts too, saying that we were lying. It was awful. We got my sister into the car and called the cops."

"Did you press charges?"

"Oh yeah, but nothing ever happened because she'd been drinking and we never found her underwear."

"Did she have a rape kit done?"

"Oh yeah, and that was just as awful."

"And did they find his semen?"

"Of course they did. There it was. It was like, hello!"

"And nothing happened?" I hate hearing these stories.

"No. Nothing ever happened to him because he changed his defense from saying that it never happened to saying that it was consensual."

"No way."

"Way. That son of a bitch and his wife were hollering that we were liars and it never happened, and then they find his semen in her and he changes his story and starts saying it was consensual. It still makes me mad and it was two years ago. Let me tell you, you could just look at this man and know that my sister, or any woman for that matter, would never have consensual sex with him. Not him. He was just gross."

"And his wife? Did she get a clue?" I ask, already knowing what to expect.

"She stood up for him the whole time."

"Jeez. What is it with these women who protect abusers? I'm sorry to say, but I think they're just as guilty." Angela nods in agreement. I think about my stepmother and how she never did anything to stop my dad. I think about my real mom and how she didn't know it was going on at all. She has told me many times before that she wished she hadn't let me go live with my dad. "Did that woman stay with him or did she divorce him?" I ask Angela.

"They went on a cruise right after that like nothing happened. I hope they had fun," she says bitterly.

"How's your sister?"

"She's doing better. She was already depressed because of our childhood, and then for this to happen, it was just awful. But she's doing OK now," Angela says but looks sad when she says it. "And you know, it didn't happen to me; it happened to her, but I still feel responsible like I should have done something. I feel like I should have known or I could have saved her, you know?"

"I know exactly how you feel," I say quietly. "I've always felt guilty that it was my dad who abused my stepsister. My dad caused her to have such low self-esteem; my dad caused her to marry abusive men. It was my dad who abused us." Angela and I stare at each other for a moment, understanding each other's pain so well.

"But all you can do is keep going and have faith," Angela says after a moment. "Maybe this movie will help. Maybe a woman in a low time in her life, or even a young girl, will see that there's light at the end of the tunnel. That things do get better no matter what you've been through and that you can lead an awesome life." Angela smiles at me and the birds above her head start chirping again.

1979

"Angie," my dad called. "Swim closer to me, honey." There were sharks in the water, and they were close to us. We were out past where the waves break. I was 7, and I was scared. "You're all right, honey. Those sharks aren't after you. Swim to me. You're safe with me." I swam as hard as I could and reached my dad. My heart was pounding. He held onto me. He could touch the bottom because he was so tall. I held onto his neck. It was just me and my dad out in the ocean with the sharks. I could see my stepmother on the shore with my stepbrother and stepsister. Ever since I was able to swim, I swam out past the waves with my dad. He taught me how to dive underneath them and lie on the bottom against the sand as they passed over my head. Sometimes when I came up for air there was another wave right away, and I had to dive back down as quickly as I could. I hated when that happened. It scared me. Then there was the threat of sharks. The sharks made me more nervous than the waves.

"It's all right, honey. I've got you. You're safe."

Dream Journal—May 13, 2001
 I dreamed about the angel picture in the alcoholic Angela's bedroom I was moving in closer to it and saw that it was actually a puzzle. The closer I got to it, the more I could see that there was a whole story in each little piece. When I stood back from it again, it looked like any other picture of an angel.

Day 14 of the search
Somewhere in Indiana

"He messed with my mind," the alcoholic Angela says and then is silent for a long time. I just sit with the phone cradled against my neck, listening to her breathe. "My dad hurt me like you wouldn't believe," she whispers like she's afraid she'll be discovered.

"What did he do?"

"I'll never tell you."

"How come?"

"Because I can't speak about it." She is silent for a moment. "He loved to brush my hair," she mumbles. "He was always in the bedroom, demanding or telling me what I had to do."

"And what would you have to do?" I get no response.

"This is a God thing, that you started calling," the alcoholic Angela says after a moment and then trails off.

"Angela, you can call me when you're sober, you know. You tell me that you didn't want to be on camera, and you didn't want me to come see you, but yet you keep calling me. Then I come see you anyway, and you say you want to be a part of this, but then you change your mind. And now you're still calling me drunk, mumbling about your dad."

"I'm an alcoholic."

"Yeah, so? Do you know how many women are going through the same thing?" I wonder if I'm being too harsh on her.

"I know. But I'm totally . . . influenced by alcohol. The only power I have is alcohol." She sucks in a breath like she can't believe she just said that out loud. "Oh my gosh."

"Well, what do you think about getting help or going to AA or rehab?" I try to keep my balance as we fly down the highway.

"Please, I've done that already too many times."

"I see that it worked for you," I joke. She cackles. "How about this then? How about you quit calling me unless you're going to call me when you're sober? How about that? Don't call me again unless you're sober." We drive past a sign that reads, "Never underestimate an American." I wonder if Angela will ever get better.

"Why don't you come back and get me and take me to California with you?" she suggests.

"I can't take you to California, Angela. I can't talk you into liking yourself either. I can't take away your past. I can't change your life for you. That's your job. I'm trying to change my own life. I can't fix yours." I am definitely being harsh. I roll my eyes. But I'm sick of being a babysitter. I hear her let out a long sigh.

"But I'm going to die."

"We're all going to die, Angela." Maybe I've been on the road too long—or received too many of these drunken phone calls. Angela Shelton is beginning to annoy me. "It's how you live your life while you're here that's the important thing." I watch Indiana glide by and wonder if I'm actually helping her or if I'm just another person on her drunk dial list. I'm frustrated and want nothing more than a cigarette. "We all have our issues, Angela."

"I know. But I can't fix mine. I don't know how."

"Help is out there, that's for sure. You just have to ask for it. If you don't get better for yourself, do it for the other Angela Sheltons. Do it for your family. But just do it. You are the only one holding you back."

"Everyone thinks I'm so great though. And I'm not."

"I think you're great too." She reminds me of how some people think I'm so successful and well put together when they don't know that I actually smack myself in the face like a crazy person. Sometimes I feel like I'm in that movie *American Beauty* where Annette Bening smacks herself over and over on the face because she didn't sell the house. And she doesn't look like the type of person to do such a thing. What I'm realizing while listening to Angela is that there's no such thing as a type of person who feels and does things to hurt herself and others. There are no boundaries. There is no perfect profile. "Angela, people think you're great because you are great. You are the only one who is fighting you, nobody else. So don't call me again unless you're sober."

My cell phone blinks out. The battery is dead. "Crap," I blurt out, thinking that she must think I hung up on her. I stare at my phone, kind of grateful for its death. I'm sick of hearing about how low life is for her, especially after meeting her and seeing how adorable she is. It's like watching someone beat herself up and being helpless to do anything about it. It's like watching myself.

1979

I was in the hallway with my stepsister and stepmother. We were outside of my dad's room. I glanced inside the room as my stepmother opened the door. I could see the heaping mass of my dad floating naked on the waterbed. He was rocking back and forth on the waves of the bed. His thingy was sticking straight up. I thought it looked funny. My stepmother touched Lisa's back, urging her to move forward into the room. Lisa looked straight ahead like she was lost or something. Once Lisa stepped into the bedroom, my stepmother shut the door. I looked up at her, wondering why I didn't get to go in there too. I curled my toes around the green shag carpet and tried to imagine what my dad was doing to Lisa in there on the waterbed.

My stepmother walked me away from the door. I went to color and wait for my sister to come out of my dad's bedroom. She looked like she was lost, like she wasn't inside her body, when she finally came out. I tried to get her to color with me, but she refused. She hated coloring.

Day 15 of the search
Angela Shelton in Kentucky

"I thought this was a scam," the Angela Shelton in Kentucky says. "And that's why I didn't call you back." She's a Caucasian blonde dentist with a cute baby voice. I caught her right when she got home from a long day at work. She owns and runs her own dental practice. "You must have self-esteem," she tells me when I ask her what she would like to say to women. I'm beginning to understand that I'm really asking what these Angelas would say to me. She has the perfect dentist smile. I would go to her if I lived here. I want my teeth to be as perfect as hers are. "Self-esteem is probably the hardest thing for people to have," Angela continues. "Everybody wants to walk around and feel that 'I'm nobody,' 'I can't do it,' 'I wish I was like her,' 'I wish I could be doing that,' or 'I wish I had that,' or 'I wish I looked like that.' We never give ourselves enough credit for who we are and what we're capable of." I feel like applauding Angela Shelton.

"You're so great. I love all these Angela Sheltons. You seem to have all the answers."

"It hasn't been easy, that's for sure. I've been doing a lot of work on myself. I used to get really angry," she admits. It's hard to picture this Angela getting angry. "I used to throw things and become violent even though I have a little voice." I try visualizing her pitching a fit, but her baby voice throws me off. I can't picture it. I see myself having fits. I've certainly thrown things and acted like a maniac and even smacked my own face, but I don't admit to that. I just stand there watching this Angela with her perfect teeth.

"But I'm past all that now. I don't have to do that anymore." Angela smiles.

"What changed?" I have a flash of smacking myself like I did when I was little. I did it when I felt stupid or when someone was trying to twist my words around and I couldn't communicate. I beat myself up. I've never told anybody that before. I wonder if this Angela Shelton ever did anything like that or if she just threw things. I don't ask. I'm still curious about how she stopped her behavior.

"Well, a lot of it came with my relationship with God," she confesses. I think about the Kansas Angela putting God first. "I've been praying and asking to grow and to change and to be a better person. That's what I'm striving to do—be a better person. And God helps me do that. She really does."

"I like that you call God a she."

"I don't believe in all the he, he, he, stuff. That's all power and control. I think a woman needs to be president too."

"No kidding. These Angela Sheltons just keep getting better and better." Angela yawns but I don't take it personally. It's late and she has to be at work by 7 a.m. and has an hour drive. "We should let you go to bed."

"I have to be up by 5 a.m. I rarely stop working."

"Are you a workaholic like me?" I think about the Missouri Angela Shelton saying she always needs to be doing something.

"I'm always working. I love what I do, and I haven't found anyone else who can do things the way I want them to be done, so I do them myself. And I've actually paid off my dental practice. I just did that recently."

"Congratulations. That's an amazing feat to get out of debt. That's awesome." Angela grins. She's proud of herself. As my crew packs up the equipment, Angela shows me her new ad in the yellow pages. It's so cool to see our name there. I make plans to meet her at her dental practice in the morning and head back to the RV. I daydream about paying off the bills for this movie and repaying all my investors like Angela paid back her loan.

We all brush our teeth really well before going to bed. I lie in the bedroom of the motor home looking up at the ceiling and suddenly I'm more grateful than nervous about being on this trip. I'm grateful that there are Angela Sheltons in the world. I think about this Angela telling me about her anger issues. I feel like these women are more together than I am. I pulled the movie together and I'm on the road pulling this off somehow with the help of my small crew, but I feel lost. I'm successful. I'm doing it; I'm directing my first movie. But I can't place where my negative thoughts come from. I wonder if I can rise to the occasion like these other Angelas. I feel like such a jerk, setting out to do this and thinking that I knew what I was doing, like I had it all planned. I'm seeing that I don't know anything. I was out to make a movie to inspire women, and I'm the one who is inspired. If everything really does happen for a reason, then these Angelas are like angels spotlighting areas in my life, guiding me toward something. I'm just not sure where I'm heading.

1980

My dad's lawyer stopped yelling at me. I didn't understand why he was so upset with me. I wanted to know what I did wrong. None of it made any sense. I wanted to scream, but I had to behave in the courtroom. I was dressed up as if it were Easter. This was a special day.

My dad looked down at the table as he sat with my step-mother and his lawyer. I stepped off the witness stand in my patent leather shoes. Someone led me out of the courtroom and into the hallway. It must have been one of my social workers, but I don't remember. I was not really in my body. Paperwork was passed back and forth and signed. I didn't have to go back to the foster home again. I was 8 years old, and my mom now had full custody of me. My mother and my grand-mother both stood up when they saw me coming. They had been told not to sit in the courtroom. They hugged me, one after the other. I was confused. I had to go on the stand and tell the lawyers what my dad did. I tried to lie. I tried to protect him, but I kept thinking that I got him in trouble.

My grandmother grinned down at me and touched my back. She had seen be on the stand before the covered up the window in the door. She had never liked my dad. She had tried to bring a pistol in her purse, but my mom had talked her out of it. That was way before metal detectors. As I walked down the corridor with my mom and my grandmother, the sound of our shoes on the linoleum reminded me of walking to the principal's office. I wondered what would happen to my step-brother and stepsister. I tried to catch a glimpse of them, but we turned the corner and left the courthouse. I didn't get to see them as children ever again.

Day 16 of the search
Angela Shelton in Kentucky

We pass a playground that sits right on the side of a four-lane road. There's no barrier between the exhaust from the cars and the children playing. We slowly inch by in the RV and watch, horrified, as one van after another passes by the playing children.

"Father, forgive them" is written across a big billboard as we turn into the parking lot of Angela Shelton's dental practice. I think of how many people live with abusers, know them, work with them, or live right beside them and don't even know it. I sigh, thinking of the Angela in South Carolina with whom I lost contact. I hope her children are OK. I hope the children in the playground will be safe. I shake my head like an Etch A Sketch like Angela in Illinois did to remove the thoughts of abuse from my mind.

We walk into Angela Shelton's dental office and find her dressed all in purple, her favorite color. She's brushing her teeth, which we all find hilarious. She gives us all toothbrushes that say "Angela Shelton" on them and pulls out her toothpaste and loads us all up. We follow orders.

"How long do you have to do this?"

"Two minutes," Angela mumbles around her toothbrush.

"Two minutes!" I'm learning more from these Angela Sheltons than I thought I would. I have to have self-esteem, be independent, not rely on a man, believe that everything happens for a reason, and brush my teeth for two minutes.

"Did you always want to be a dentist?"

"I wanted to be a vet first."

"There's an Angela Shelton who's a vet," I mumble through my toothpaste.

"I grew up on a farm and was always around animals. I love animals and I grew up tough. I was raised like one of the boys. I had a job making tires too."

"No. You?"

"Hard to believe, I know. But don't let my little voice fool you," she smiles. "But I became a dentist. A smile is everything. And when you smile, I smile, and then it just passes on." My crew and I smile at her as if it's an order. "Ever since I was little, I used to make my dad lean back on his chair and I'd inspect his mouth. My dad was my first patient," Angela explains proudly. It makes me think of my dad. He was my first at a few things too, but I shake that thought out of my mind.

Angela has no abusive past. She grew up with a great family, and all she wants to do is help others. "I don't like to see anyone hurting. And if you think about it, if we all do our part, however small, to make the world a better place, then it will be a better place." She tells us how she's the only dentist in her county who contributes her services to people who don't have insurance. "It would break my heart to turn people away because they didn't have any money. I just couldn't live with myself." I wonder if all the Angela Sheltons have the same save-the-world complex. So far they are all caretakers in some way. I wish I could inject the self-esteem of this Angela Shelton into the alcoholic Angela.

1985

I was 13 when I wanted to kill myself the most. I didn't take any pills or cut my wrists with a razor. I had a machete. I was going to plunge it into my heart violently. I was in the room I shared with my mother in our apartment in San Diego. She was going out with a man who had a lot of weapons. He had knives, throwing blades, all kinds of things. He was really into martial arts. He left his things lying around, and I had one of his knives. My mom was at work. It was around 3 p.m. I was home from school, and I wanted to die. I was just done. I couldn't take my inner pain anymore because I couldn't name it or explain it, and I didn't know where it was coming from.

I looked into the mirror with the knife held to my chest. I thought I was being a little too overdramatic about the whole thing. I wondered if I could even go through with it. The TV was on in the living room, and I heard Oprah Winfrey. She was talking about how she had been abused as a child. I stared into the mirror and listened. Then I lowered the knife and walked down the hall to the living room. It was just me and Oprah, and she was talking about how she had been abused too. I couldn't believe it. I put the knife back where I found it. If Oprah Winfrey could go through hell and get to where she was, I thought I could do something with my life too. I figured I was a real jerk if I killed myself. I stared at Oprah's face on the TV and swore that one day I would meet her. I would thank her for saving my life simply by telling her story. Maybe I could do the same thing for someone else one day.

Day 17 of the search
Angela Shelton in Ohio

"This is interesting but strange." The Angela Shelton in Ohio thinks I'm nuts. She seems annoyed that my crew and I are here. It took more calls to her than to any other Angela to reach her. She sounded skeptical over the phone and now she looks skeptical in person as she walks out into the lobby to meet us. She shows us around her veterinary office. I'm going to try to get this over with as quickly as I can, so I start the questions before we even have her seated. I don't want to cut any Angela Shelton out—they should all be in the movie!—even though this one seems eager for us to leave.

"What would you say to women, to girls who want to do what you're doing? Do you have any advice for them?"

"Um, to go out and do anything you want to do. If you work hard enough at it, you can do it. I never thought I could make it through vet school, to be honest with you, and I did." I tell her a little bit about my story and the different Angelas with whom I've spoken. She nods and stares at me. "Nothing bad like that ever happened to me."

"Is there anything you would change about the world if you could?"

"I'd like to see everybody have a place to live and someone to love them." That's all she says. She looks around at us. I'm not sure how to engage her.

"Are you happy with your life right now?"

"Yes. I have a great boyfriend. He rides a motorcycle. That is really fun. We go on great rides together." Her demeanor totally changes when she talks about her boyfriend.

"What makes you sad or angry?"

"Seeing animals mistreated. And it does make me very angry hearing about other women being abused like you said. That's not right, and that makes me angry—even though nothing like that ever happened to me." She fidgets. I figure that she has to get back to work and I've taken up enough of her time. My crew and I pack up and head out of Ohio. We are all tired and hungry and ready for the Angela in Detroit, who is our next destination.

1978

I never knew when my dad would fly off the handle. One minute he could be fun and relaxed and the next minute he was in a rage. When he flew into a rage, he usually let me know what was coming. He wanted me to know how he was going to beat me. The anticipation of a whipping was sometimes worse than the actual beating. I hid under the bed most of the time when my father was in one of his rages. I could hear his feet pounding on the floor as he searched the house for me. He'd already gotten Steve and Lisa with his belt. He had punched a big hole through Steve's door with his fist. I was next. My dad stepped into my room. I could see his feet turn and head toward the bed. I held my breath.

"Angie?" I didn't make a peep. His feet spread apart and his body came into view and then his big head. He found me. "Honey, come on out of there. I'm not going to hurt you." I followed his orders. You had to do what my dad said.

I crawled out from under the bed. He helped me not knock my head on the bed railing. He didn't beat me. He kept his promise. I was confused. It seemed unfair that my stepbrother and stepsister were whipped and I wasn't, but I was thankful to be free from pain for the moment. My dad hugged me. I was happy not to get his belt, but I felt strange. I wondered if my dad was crazy.

Day 18 of the search
Angela Shelton in Detroit

I have never seen so many liquor stores on one street in my entire life. As we drive through Detroit there is a liquor store or a pawnshop on practically every single corner. The alcoholic

Angela Shelton pops into my mind for a moment, but Detroit pulls me back to the present as we move through the nastiest streets I've ever seen. I've been to all kinds of places throughout the world, but Detroit takes the cake for the worst neighborhoods. I find it a perfect fit that the most religious Angela lives here. Maybe she's here to raise the energy a notch.

We drive over train tracks and suddenly there are manicured hedges and sprinkler systems. "Talk about being on the other side of the tracks." I've heard that term, but I've never seen it literally play out. We cross another set of tracks and the houses get worse again. We turn off of a main drag lined with liquor stores and make our way through a neighborhood that looks like it might be winning the ghetto battle. Angela Shelton's house is at the end of the block. Kids start streaming out of their houses, eyes bugging out and mouths agape at five white folks in a huge RV moving down their street.

The Detroit Angela Shelton is a large-breasted African-American woman dressed in pink. She's on the sidewalk with her mouth dropped open just like everyone else. She keeps putting her hand on her head like she's in shock. She looks me up and down as I step out of the RV. We both start grinning and hugging each other.

"Oh my goodness," Angela says over and over. "I kept telling my husband that ya'll were coming and he didn't believe me, and now look at this big ole thing," she says, pointing to the RV. More neighbors pour out of their homes, and curious kids inch in closer. "Who are you?" Angela asks one kid. "I ain't never seen some of these people before," she tells me and then turns back to the group of kids. "Ya'll are just seeing this movie camera out and want to get all up in my business." The kids laugh with her and mock for the camera. "Oh my goodness." The crowd grows bigger around her. "They're making a movie about me," she explains to a nosy neighbor as her husband comes around the corner. "This is my husband, Gregory." Angela waves to him. Gregory smiles shyly. Angela turns toward him and speaks very clearly. "See, I told you they were coming."

I wonder why she makes such an effort to speak directly to him like that but then realize he is deaf when he signs back to her as he says, "I didn't believe it. But this is crazy." He looks the RV up and down. Angela laughs hysterically. Gregory shyly waves goodbye and heads to the back of the house again.

"He's back there working on his truck." Angela shakes her head as she looks at the camera. "What are you looking at?" she asks the group of mingling kids. "Ya'll go on. You've been on camera enough." She turns back to me. "I haven't seen half those kids before, can you believe it?" The kids run off but stay within sight of the camera. "I thought you were lying at first, but God always has a plan." Angela looks at the group of kids and shakes her head, laughing. We stand there in front of her house smiling at each other. I feel like I've known this Angela Shelton forever.

"You're such an inspiration to me."

"Me? Why?"

"Why? Because of all that you've been through. I mean, we were on the phone for hours." I am so excited to meet her. Then I realize that I'm the only one who knows her history. I've heard it over the phone, but I need her to repeat it for the camera so my crew and the audience can hear what I've heard. "I want to hear your story. I want you to tell me about your life."

"I've had it rough, but I have a good life now. Jesus said, 'Walk by faith and not by sight.' If you live your life for God, things just work out."

"I feel like that's what I'm doing right now with this movie."

"You are. You don't know how many you will help, but you will help many and you just have to keep that faith and keep moving forward. Walk by faith and not by sight and trust that God has got your back. It's hard though," she says just as I'm thinking that sounds easier said than done. "I have hard days too. It's hard to keep these bills paid."

"I hear that. I'm so stressed out my shoulders are like earrings."

Angela laughs and swats the air like she knows exactly what I'm talking about. "You just wake up and give your day to God. Put yourself in God's court. Sometimes life slaps you upside the head, Angie, but you just keep stepping out on faith no matter what. I'm a woman of God and I know I'm protected," she says with such conviction that I believe her. I wish I had that kind of certainty. "It's like when I teach my Sunday school class. We play this game where I blindfold the kids and one of them has to lead the others. I tell them that if they're leading, they better remember they have a lot of people waiting to be led in the right direction, so they better know where they're going."

"Speaking about going somewhere, I told you about my dad, right? That he's a child molester."

"Oh yeah," Angela sighs, remembering our long phone conversation.

"And I'm going to go see him," I tell her just to hear myself say it out loud.

"You're going to see him?"

"Yeah, there's an Angela Shelton in his town. And you know what she does for a living?"

"What?"

"She tracks sexual predators." Angela's mouth is agape. "That's what I said." I mimic her mouth falling open, and we both laugh.

"But you're going to go see him?" she repeats to make sure she heard that correctly.

"Yes, I am. It's kind of weird that there's an Angela Shelton in his town—like I'm meant to go or something. I think I have to go."

"The Lord is leading you there. When was the last time you saw your dad?"

"When I was 14. I saw him very briefly two years ago, but the last time I really visited was when I was 14. Then when I was 18 I went back to the town we lived in and picked up all the court papers from when we went to court."

"You had to go to court with your dad?" Angela asks and shifts her weight to her other hip.

"Yeah," I sigh, deciding not to explain it all. "And I took the court papers to my grandfather, my dad's dad, because I thought he would do something. I thought he'd help stop my dad."

"Your granddad?"

"Yeah. Because my dad had married another woman who had kids." Angela lets out a slow sigh. "I brought the papers to my grandfather, but my grandparents told me that what happened was water under the bridge and they wished me luck, but they didn't want me to call them ever again, not to come by there, not to write them, and when they die, not to come to their funeral."

"They did not say that to you."

"They did."

"That's crazy." Angela moves her head from side to side like she's trying to find a place to fit that information into her head.

"That's denial for you. And I'm their only grandchild or was at that point."

"You know, I was molested too," Angela says after a moment of silence, and it's my turn to be shocked.

"No, you only told me that you were raped."

"Well, that's a whole other story." Angela waves at the air. "But when I was 3, the neighbor boy was molesting me in the yard and trying to get his thing in there, you know? And luckily my mother was watching out the window and came running out and beat that kid off of me."

"Yea for good mothers."

"I heard that. I have a great mother. I look back now and see that I really gave her a hard time. She didn't even know I had been raped until much later. We had this thing in our church, the boundary classes where it teaches you to have boundaries."

"I need one of those classes."

"Doesn't everybody?" Angela swats the air and laughs. "But I told the congregation how I was raped at gunpoint. I came out and told the whole church, and my mother had never heard that and I think that really hurt her. And then my sister came out and told everybody that she'd been raped too."

"Jeez. That must have been a hard day at church."

"Yeah. Women don't tell when they go through something like that. They just don't talk about it."

"I know. That's why I'm doing this movie, to find out how women are doing and to give them an opportunity to talk. And most of the Angelas have experienced some kind of abuse, but a lot of them don't want to be on camera."

"I could see that and I understand that. When you first called me I was wondering if I wanted to be telling my business to the world. But I believe that God sent you calling and I answered. We have to talk about it. The guy who raped me got away with it. That was date rape, and he got away." She looks off into the distance.

"Most men get away with it. My father was never caught."

"But this is good. This is good to talk. We need to speak the truth. I knew I was meant to meet you. I knew that God sent you, but who knew God would send a skinny white girl?" We both look at each other and howl with laughter.

"Well, I've always wanted to be a black woman."

"Get out. Why? Because we're so strong?"

"That's it. I admire you. And I don't mean it to be insulting at all. I just always wanted that strength, the strength of the black woman. It takes a lot to be a woman period, but add being African-American and it's a whole other ball game."

"Oppression hurts. But you're right—we are strong. You just made me think of my first experience with racism, where someone at work referred to me as 'you people,' and I thought I am not 'you people.' I am Angela Shelton." She grins at me. "And you should be careful how you entertain others because you could be entertaining an angel."

"Or an Angela," I add.

"Right! An angel or an Angela. And it doesn't matter whether she's a big ole black woman or a skinny white girl." Angela nudges me with her elbow, and we both giggle. I love her.

Day 19 of the search
Angela Shelton in Detroit

God freaks me out. Church makes me uncomfortable. When I was little, the people who preached that they knew the truth about God beat and molested us. I have always had disdain and fear of religion. I don't trust it. I don't trust people in power who claim to know God. They make me feel ill at ease and on guard. I use words like Universe and the Divine instead of God. But when my crew and I go back to Angela's house in the morning, she takes us to church with her, and I decide to release judgment and fear and just feel the energy and not label it. I sing along with the choir and feel alive with the gospel music ringing in my ears. My skin feels tingly. I feel the love and connection. It is as if we're all one voice.

I meet Angela's mother. She hugs me and thanks me for making this movie. I remember Angela telling me how her mother didn't even learn about Angela's rape until years later. Angela's mom makes me think of my own mom. "I'm proud of Angela, and I'm proud of you," she says.

After we spend four hours at church singing and praising, a bunch of Angela's choir sisters come back to her house to watch her being filmed for the movie. They hover as we point the camera at Angela and her husband. I ask her how her life is now. "My marriage is hard. It's hard. I have a husband who is deaf, and it seems like I have to work harder than I would have to if I had a husband who had his hearing. But it works out." I look over at Gregory.

"What do you think about that?" I ask him.

"Oh, don't be fooled. He reads lips, and he's real good at it too," Angela warns and nudges him. "The Lord blessed me with Greg. He really did."

"My life with Angie is like a fairy tale that will never end," Gregory tells us and sneaks a peek at her. "I'm very happy to have her as a wife and a friend and a lover." Angela elbows him. "She changed my life. She opened me up." Gregory looks at Angela out of the corner of his eye. I hope that someday I can meet a man who loves me like that.

"What do you think about what I'm doing?" I ask him.

"I think it's exciting, talking about different Angela Sheltons. It helps bring out the other Angela Sheltons with one going around looking for the others." I think about all the Angela Sheltons who won't come forward, who keep canceling and changing their minds about being in this movie. I wonder if Gregory is right, that this will help bring them out too. "It helps a lot," he assures me. "It helps us to understand more about each other." I wonder if he has a better idea of the movie than I do.

I look over at Angela and wonder if she'll talk about her rape. She told me about it over the phone, but there hasn't been a good time to bring it up on camera yet. All of her choir sisters are mingling around the living room, and I don't know if this is the best time. I look at her. She looks back at me.

"Do you want to talk about your rape?" I ask her point-blank. Her choir sisters and her husband suddenly have to go find something in the kitchen all at once. As the mass exit happens, Angela looks around and half laughs.

"Nope," she blurts out. Then just as quickly says, "Yep, I'll talk about the rape." She takes a deep breath as the room clears out and she is left alone with me, my crew, and the camera. "I was dating a man. We went out a couple times, and the third time I went out with him . . ." She goes back to the memory for a moment. "I suppressed a lot of this. I forgot about the gun to my head and all of that. I thought I was over it. I didn't realize that I still had some feelings about that."

Her face begins to reveal the feelings she's talking about. "I never told anybody because I thought it was my fault." Angela looks up at the ceiling, going back to that day in her mind. "I just remember the first couple of times we dated he was kind of aggressive, and I didn't like him like that. And the last time we dated, the time he raped me, he put a gun to my head. And the thing that really messed me up was that he took me to an apartment building that one of my cousins lived in and she was right next door and I couldn't call and ask anybody for help. But what I look at now is the strength I had in the midst of being raped and violated. I just acted like nothing was going on because he was holding a gun to my head."

She falls into a faraway silence. None of us know what to do. We're all staring at her face, which is filled with emotion for the first time since we met. A tear finds a path down her cheek. Neither of us says anything for a moment. She looks at me, expecting another question.

"I have a request. Can I hear that song you all sang at church."

"Hey, you guys," Angela calls out, happy for the change of subject. "She wants to hear our song." Angela's fellow gospel singers come out from their hiding places and gather around her. Angela grins at me as the women find their places around her.

"Look at all these amazing women. I wish I was a black woman," I say to bring some levity back into the room. The women howl with laughter. Angela's mother is bent over giggling. She stands up and looks at me and points.

"You're black," she announces like she's performing a knighting ceremony. I nod and thank her and hope I serve my sisters well.

Angela starts singing first, and the women come in on the chorus. It is one of the greatest gospel songs I have ever heard. "God specializes in the impossible" is the chorus, and it's imprinted on the minds of my crew and me forever. I feel that some of Angela Shelton's faith has rubbed off on me. God really does specialize in the impossible.

Dream Journal—May 23, 2001

I dreamed that a huge red apple rolled down Fifth Avenue toward me and stopped at my feet.

Dream Journal—May 25, 2001

I keep having that dream of riding the tricycle and pulling the RV behind me. I dreamed the same dream again last night but I was no longer pulling the RV; I was lounging in a lawn chair on top of it as it sailed down the highway without any wheels. The lawn chair folded and had that plastic ribbing that sticks to you and makes lines all over your back. I assume this dream has a good message. I hope it does.

Day 27 of the search
Angela Shelton in New York

My crew and I have been in New York City for days now. We stopped to take a break and visit friends while I was hunting down money. There were a few investor prospects here, but they fell through. I've cleaned out my IRA already to keep everyone fed. My accountant said I was nuts, but I can't stop now. I have more Angela Sheltons to meet. I've cashed out my savings and sold my stocks. I'm now down to $50 and I'm not joking. I haven't told my crew just how bad it is. I keep hearing the Detroit

Angela Shelton in my head saying to walk by faith and not by sight. I wonder if I'm walking the line of faith or delusion as I check my balance again.

We pass a billboard that reads, "What's In A Name?" on the way to Queens to meet the New York Angela Shelton. I didn't really research my name. I just know it means angel, daughter of God, and messenger of God. We pull up in front of Angela's house, park, and the crew follows me up her walkway. She has a sign hanging on her metal-gated door that says, "With God." Daisy, Angela's mother, answers the door, and we fall in love instantly. She is a round, jolly African-American woman who is constantly praying. She prays for us when she answers the door; she prays for the babies that fill the cribs that line her living room; and she prays when she introduces me to Angela Shelton. Daisy looks after the neighbors' babies while they work. She has a lot of neighbors and a lot of babies. They're all bright eyed and adorable. The whole room is happy, and Jesus is everywhere. There are pictures of him, quotes from him, and his name is on Daisy's lips every minute. I half expect him to come walking into the room any minute.

Angela Shelton stands there grinning with her long braids dangling on her shoulders while her mother fusses over the babies and us. The New York Angela Shelton is fierce. She is covered shoulder to ankle in denim and sparkles with glitter. Her gold tooth shines when she smiles. I love her immediately. "Hello, Miss Angela Shelton," she says. I want to jump up and down for joy and praise Jesus.

"I'm so excited. This is so exciting." We just grin at each other. Angela's 11-year-old daughter peeks around the corner before coming into the room. Angela puts her arm around her.

"This is my daughter, Melissa. She is so excited to meet you."

"Hey, Melissa." I go to hug her, but Angela puts out her hand to stop me.

"Hold up, she's got strep," Angela warns. "She had to stay home from school today, but she had to get out of bed to meet Miss Angela Shelton. Ain't that right, baby?" Angela squeezes her daughter, who does nothing but grin. "You should've seen her when you first called me. She said, 'Oh, Mommy, aren't you going to call that lady back? She sounds so nice.'"

"Are you talking about me leaving messages?" I remember leaving quite a few.

"Yes. She said you sounded so nice on the phone and that she liked your voice."

"Really? That's funny; I've always hated my voice. I even loathe hearing myself on an answering machine."

"God gave your voice to you so therefore it is beautiful," Daisy calls out from behind me. I turn and smile at her. "Cherish your voice and yourself. It's from God, and what God makes is wonderful."

"Thank you, Daisy. You have a good point." I figure that most everything Daisy Shelton says must be true. I don't know why. I just have a feeling.

"It's true," she confirms, reading the back of my head. "You're a beautiful light of God. I could tell there was something about you and these people." She gestures toward my crew, which is standing there wondering what to do next. "All of ya'll are here for God. I can tell it. You're working for the Lord and the Lord is guiding you. You are doing God's work by making this movie."

I don't know whether I am delusional or depressed, but meeting all these Angelas has made me think that I am doing something worthwhile and that it will all work out. I grin, thinking about that meeting where I shared this idea for the first time and talked about matching Angela Shelton hats and jackets. Who knew it would be more like matching lives.

"You ready to make me into a movie star?" Angela asks. She is glossed and glittering. We move outside to film the New York Angela Shelton. "What would you say to women?" I ask her once the camera is recording.

"Stay strong and keep a level head." She giggles and her gold tooth shines.

"What do you think about the fact that a lot of the Angelas I've talked to have been raped, beaten, or molested?"

"Whoo wee." She breathes out and shakes her head. "You know something? That almost happened to me." I'm floored. She hadn't mentioned that during our phone calls.

"Really?"

"Yes. I was almost raped one time."

"How old were you?"

"That was many years ago." She waves her hand in the air. "I was like 19 or 20—19."

"What happened?" I lean over to check the camera to be sure the tape is rolling. Gallo nods at me.

"My best friend, Judy, and I were coming home from the movies and we were going to the liquor store. On the way down the street, we passed this guy we knew." Angela looks up in the sky like she is seeing it all over again. "When we came out of the liquor store, I told my friend that I didn't want to pass by that guy again. I didn't have a good feeling about him, you know? And my friend said, 'Oh, that's so-and-so. Everybody knows him.' And I said, 'I don't care who it is. I don't like him.' But we passed by him anyway." Angela rolls her eyes like she is still annoyed at herself for not listening to her gut. "So we passed by him, and as we passed I got this awful feeling in my stomach."

"You knew it was going to happen?"

"Exactly. And sure enough, here comes the guy and he was like, 'Yo yo yo,' and he put his hand into his jacket. I thought he had a gun, so I grabbed my friend and tried to run, but he ran behind me and grabbed me and drug me into the park." She smacks her lips together as if still to this day she would love to sock him one in the face. "And from there I was just fighting for my life because I thought he was trying to rob me, but he was going up my dress. He ripped my shirt. That was the worst experience I ever had in my life, but see, he couldn't get none because my friend didn't leave me. And she's short! She's so short." Angela looks over at Sylvia. "She's shorter than you," she points out and laughs. "And she didn't run. She stayed there with me and we just kept fighting him and fighting him until he couldn't take no more."

I want to cheer. I think of how so many women don't look out for each other like that. I love Angela Shelton even more. I want her as my friend.

"And you know what? We went past that liquor store on our way back, and I'm walking with one boob hanging out because I told you he tore my shirt. I was a mess, and my friend was a mess, and we passed by that liquor store. There's this girl standing there that we had passed earlier and she asks, 'What happened?'" Angela mimics her voice. "And you know I hauled off and punched that girl right in her face. Because she heard. She was right there and she heard what was going on. It was right there in front of her, and she didn't do anything, didn't call the cops or anything, so I punched her." Angela laughs, showing off her gold tooth again.

"Wow."

"All of us females should stick together. Unity. We don't have that." She shakes her head from side to side and her gold jewelry sparkles with her glitter.

"Why not?"

"Why?" Angela looks at me like she's trying to figure that out for herself. "I don't know why females are the way they are. Because I believe in unity. We need to teach women to look out for each other. We need a club. I'm serious. What if we all stuck together and took care of all the rapists and child molesters. Put them all into one room and let the women decide what to do with them. I bet you we'd come up with something good." She grins.

"What is it that keeps you so strong? That's what I would like to know."

"My daughter. She keeps me strong. She gives me the will to go on no matter what, and as long as she's here, that's my motivation."

"Nice. Did she see your husband abuse you ever?" Angela had told me on the phone about her abusive ex. It was the rape story that I wasn't prepared for.

"Yeah, she saw it. But I got out of that. I didn't let that go on." I think of her punching the girl at the liquor store, and I believe her. "We get on good now, me and him. We're friends. That took a while. He sends his child support, but when we were together he was like a time bomb; you never knew when it was going to go off. I was one of the strong-minded women to get out of it though. I didn't stay around saying to myself, 'Oh, he's going to change. He's just like this for now.' I didn't try to find excuses for him. Because it doesn't matter if something is bothering him at the time or whatever—it's not right. No woman should stand for that or go through that. But as long as their self-esteem is low, they'll stick with it. Because they feel that 'Oh, I don't have an education.' or 'Oh, I don't have no place to go. Oh, he's the only one that I've been with. He does love me.' No, no. You've got to get out and get away and not stand for that." Angela Shelton is like a wise sage with a gold tooth.

"You are so awesome."

"Thank you. I know." I wish I had her confidence.

"All the Angela Sheltons are so great. Look at you, what you've been through and how fierce you are. It's inspirational. All of you are inspiring me for sure."

"But you're inspiring us too, Angela. You're the one making the movie."

I don't tell her that I have $50 in my account and, in fact, do not know what I'm doing. I just smile and want to believe her. My cell phone rings and I see that it is my friend Heidi back in Los Angeles. She told me she was going to try to track down some money for me. My heart jumps for a moment, thinking that she may have succeeded. I excuse myself for one second and walk off down the street to answer it.

"I got you some money," Heidi says when I pick up.

"Oh my God, I love you. Are you serious? It couldn't come at a more perfect time."

"Marcus Allen is investing in your movie. He's an old friend of mine and I've been telling him about you since you left. I just had a long sit down with him and told him about all the Angelas you're meeting. But when I told him about your dad, he was like, 'I'm in.' He's sending you $10,000 today. I need your account number."

I almost start crying when I head back to the crew to let them know that they will be fed. "Was us eating actually in question?" Gallo wants to know. He's beside himself with excitement that it's Marcus Allen who's investing.

"I have a question though. Who is Marcus Allen?" I ask innocently. I forgot to ask Heidi that.

"What? Angela, he is only one of the best football players ever. Only you, Ang, would have Marcus Allen invest in your film and not even know who he is. You are amazing, ridiculous, or just extremely lucky."

"She's blessed is what she is," Daisy says as she comes outside and hugs me. Angela ran in to tell her the news after I got off the phone. "You are doing God's work and you will be protected all the way to the end. You just need to trust that you are taken care of. I'll be praying for you, Angela Shelton."

1978

"Ya'll get your clothes off," my dad ordered as Steve, Lisa, and I crawled into the back of his van. He was up front with my stepmother and told her to slide out of her panties as we disrobed in the back. We were on our way to another nudist colony. "I don't want anybody making fun of anybody else's body," my dad ordered as he played with my stepmother's crotch. She reached over and stroked his big thingy while he drove. Me and my stepbrother and stepsister sat naked on the mattress in the back of my dad's van as we made our way to the camp. "Now if any of you feel uncomfortable there, you just let us know," my dad told us. But once we arrived we were not allowed to put our clothes on.

I noticed a lot of ladies were wearing their underwear when we got there, so I went in search of my dad to ask him if I could put my panties on too. He was in the pool hall with a bunch of other naked fat guys. They all looked alike as they smiled down at me as I walked in. "What is it, honey?" My dad nodded to his buddies like I was so cute.

"I wanted to know if I could put my underwear on? I saw other ladies—"

I stopped talking because I knew I was in trouble just by the look on my dad's face. He leaned his pool stick against the wall and came toward me with his thingy swinging between his legs under his big belly. He grabbed me by the shoulders and walked me outside away from earshot of his naked pool mates.

"You are going to keep your clothes off, young lady, you hear me?" I nodded. I heard him. I stayed outside and watched him walk back to grab his pool stick and laugh with his bare buddies. It was his turn to knock in some balls. I wondered what other kids do when they had a dad like mine. I figured it would be hard to run away naked. I hunched my shoulders and walked off naked to see what the other naked kids were doing. I made a mental note that men were liars as I kicked up dirt with my bare feet.

Day 29 of the search
Angela Shelton in New York City

"I figured out the movie!" I announce to my crew as they file into the RV. "I have to confront my dad!" The crew looks at me like I'm nuts. "I meet all the Angelas and hear their stories, but it is through their stories and learning what we're all going through as women that I am urged to go see my dad. It just fits that way." They all look at me deadpan.

"Duh," Gallo pipes in first. "Are you telling us something we didn't already know? Of course you're going to your dad."

"We have to go see the boogeyman," Gio says. "I even brought my tomahawk." He searches through his stuff and lifts an actual tomahawk out of one of his bags. I'm dumbfounded. "When you told me your story and that there were some Angela Sheltons in your dad's state and one in his town, I knew we'd end up going to see him. I only took this job so I could go see the boogeyman."

"You have to confront him, even if we're not there with you," Chantal points out. "You have to at least go there to see him. I mean come on, you have to."

"Forget that. We're going to be there and we're going to film it," Gallo jumps in. He gets up and walks to the calendar we have pinned on the fridge. He flips the page over from May to June and stares at it for a moment. "Hey, Ang," he says quietly. "Did you see when we're going to be in South Carolina?"

"Yeah, in June."

"But did you see that we're getting there on Father's Day?" I feel nauseated.

"No." Did I just hear that correctly? "When is Father's Day?" It's such an uncelebrated day in my life that I don't even know when it is.

"Ang, we're going to arrive in your dad's town on Father's Day. That's just too weird."

"Oh my God, it's like we were totally meant to leave when we did." Chantal jumps up and looks at the calendar over Gallo's shoulder. "This is an everything-happens-for-a-reason moment."

We all sit there letting this sink in. Giovanni holds his tomahawk. I rest my hand on my Angela Shelton binder and take a deep breath. Sylvia looks like she's going to cry and Chantal stares at the calendar while Gallo grins. It's my turn to drive. I climb behind the wheel and back the motor home out. I think I'm watching all the mirrors, but I catch the back fender on something and rip the side fender of the RV off. My mind is elsewhere.

1979

My stepbrother could walk on water. Lisa and I sat on the edge of the lake and watched him do it. He was 12 going on 13 and I loved him. I didn't care that he gave us piggyback rides in exchange for getting the white stuff to shoot out of his thingy like my dad did. I wanted to please my brother during our after-school games. I wanted him to like me as much as he liked my stepsister. But I could never compare to my stepsister. My dad and my stepbrother wanted her more. She was better. I was the rotten one.

I tried many times to swim out to my stepbrother in the middle of the lake to the magical place that rose out of the bottom, but I never made it that far. Fear of the wide-open space in the lake stopped me. I couldn't see the bottom. The uncertainty about where that small mountain of land was in the middle was too much for me to bear. My stepsister never made it either. Only my stepbrother found the place in the middle of the lake that allowed him to walk on water.

Day 30 of the search
Angela Shelton in Philadelphia

Angela Shelton isn't home. We wait around and walk up and down the street to kill time. We end up finding all her neighbors instead. They come out of their doors, lean out of their windows, and some of them start following us down the street. They keep asking what five white folks are doing around this neighborhood and wonder if we aren't crazy. When I tell them about the movie we're doing, word spreads like wildfire. A group of young girls collects around us.

"I'm Angela Shelton, I'm Angela Shelton, I'm Angela Shelton!" they all yell and flail their arms about to get our attention. The national statistics cross my mind as I laugh with this adorable group of girls. The numbers claim that one out of four of these girls will be sexually abused before she turns 18. I look into their little faces and wonder if that number isn't higher.

We wait around for a while longer, but Angela Shelton stands us up.

Day 31 of the search
Somewhere in West Virginia

"Any common threads so far?" Angela Shelton in Georgia asks me once I get her on the phone. I'm calling to warn her that we're getting closer.

"Besides the fact that we're all women?" We both laugh. "Almost half are white and half African-American, and there's a Muslim in New Mexico who has eight kids. I'm trying to find a teenager but haven't had any luck. I've called a bunch of schools, but that's hard because they think you're a crazy person and aren't allowed to give that information out anyway."

"And you told me that a lot of the Angelas had been abused too, right?"

"Yes."

"I think so many women are abused that we don't even know about because people don't talk about it. I bet there are even Angelas who haven't said anything."

"There's one who was being beaten by her mother and doesn't want to talk about it because her mother is being nice to her now. There's the one who is high up in the government and wants all of my credentials to prove that I'm not stalking her. There are ones who were raped and don't want to talk on camera. There's the one who was raped in the military. There is one who was beaten and is scared to talk. There's the one who was molested by her grandfather, and the list goes on and on. There is even one who says that this movie was her idea. One Angela Shelton shouted at me to never call her again before she slammed the phone down."

"Did she really? Well, thank God I was spoiled rotten and had a happy childhood. I'm one of the rare ones, it seems. But I do know plenty of people who went through hell."

"We all know someone, it seems."

"Yes, we do. Even if you don't know that you know, you do know someone, you know?" She giggles. "When do you think you'll get here?"

"Um, well." I look at the calendar and see Father's Day circled. "We're going to get to you right after we see my dad."

"Oh my," Angela says, mirroring what I'm thinking. I take a deep breath and wish I had a cigarette. "You're going to see him? Didn't he abuse you?"

"That's the one. Good ole Papa."

"Do you think he'll freak out on you? Are you going to make sure that you're safe?"

I think about Gio and his tomahawk when I say, "I'll be fine. I'm not worried. I'm more worried about not being able to speak."

"Like freezing up? The whole flight, fight, or freeze?"

"Exactly." These Angela Sheltons know what they are talking about.

1978

My dad was a wimp. He put on a big charade, but he was a wimp. He hid behind his La-Z-Boy, but he was too fat to fit. Lisa and Steve's real father was coming up the front steps in a rage. There was a fight about to happen, and my father was revealing his pitiful side. My stepsister had told her real dad about how my dad placed her hand onto his penis. My dad started playing his games soon after I moved in with him and his new family. He started walking around naked all the time. When I was 3 and Lisa was 5, he carried her sleeping body up the stairs while he was butt naked and her hand fell and touched his penis. It woke her up for a second and she jerked her hand away as he carried her into the bedroom that I shared with her. But my father reached down and placed her hand back onto his penis and made her keep it there.

I didn't know that happened until later. What I did know was that right after that night he carried her to bed, he started telling us all to get naked with him. He never did that when he was with my mom and me. He said he wanted this new family to be comfortable with each other. My stepmother always did as he said and instructed us to do the same.

It took Lisa a long time to tell her real dad what my dad had done. Even then, she didn't tell him the half of it. But when she did tell the small detail that she did, her real dad got spitting mad. He was coming to kick my dad's butt, and my dad was shaking in his britches. My dad roared at us to get out of the room. I figured he didn't want us to see him get whipped. We hid for cover. I couldn't see if Lisa's dad got a swing in or not. I heard a lot of yelling, and I could see part of my dad's body cowering behind his recliner. That was the first time I'd ever seen my dad weak.

As I hid at a safe distance trying to see the action, I realized that my dad only beat us because we were little. Once we were big, there was nothing he could do to us. I liked how Lisa's dad was protecting her. I liked how he yelled at my dad. I wondered if my dad would protect me like that ever, but then I remembered that he was the one who hurt me the most. I held my Wonder Woman doll and imagined that I was as big and as strong as she was. I was going to stand up for little kids like me.

Dream Journal—June 1, 2001

I keep dreaming about a huge crowd of women filling the streets. Each one of them has an air of bravery and courage as if they've been through a war and won. They are dancing and laughing. It's a big crowd of women with good men surrounding them, like a protective shield. I wake up every time wondering where I was in the crowd. I never see myself, but I know I'm in there somewhere. The dream makes me think about my mother and how she always told me how important dreams are and the meanings they have. I've had this dream about five times now since January.

Day 32 of the search
Angela Shelton in Virginia

"When I see a big ole RV pulling up in front of my house, I think it must be Angela Shelton!" Angela Shelton in Virginia teases as she makes her way down her driveway. She's an adorable African-American woman who is dressed in bright yellow, which fits her jolly nature. I climb down the motor home steps and give her a big hug. "It's so good to finally meet you. I've been waiting!"

"And you're moved in." I gesture to the For Sale sign in the front yard of her new house. I want to take a Sharpie to it and write, "Bought by an amazingly independent woman." I already know her story and understand what a feat it is that she now owns her home. I hug her again. My crew hooks up the microphone and aims the camera at her once we're all in her house. She sits surrounded by boxes.

"I feel bad about all the boxes," she shrugs apologetically.

"Oh please, they symbolize so much. I love it. For me it says freedom."

"OK then. It's so good to meet you," she chuckles. "I think we just clicked on the phone. We just started talking and kept on talking. When we hung up I wondered if this was some weird joke. I just told my whole life to somebody who shared my name. But I haven't stopped talking about you since you called. I've told everyone at work too."

"What do you think about what I'm doing?"

"I think it's neat that you're going around meeting all these women. Sometimes talking to different women about what they've been through helps your life."

"You certainly have a story to tell." She stops grinning.

"I don't want to talk about that."

"Why not?"

"Because it's history, and I'm so over that."

"But you have such a great story. You're such an inspiration."

"An inspiration?"

"You're an inspiration to me. Look at what you've been through and where you're at now." I motion around her house. I know she came from an abusive relationship. I know what it took for her to be able to have her own house and be safe in it.

"No, I think you're the inspiration. Look at what you're doing." She gestures toward the camera. "See, I give it to you and you give it right back to me. We're reflecting it back on each other." She giggles.

"What would you say to other women going through the same thing?" I want to pull her story out of her. I should have recorded all the phone calls in the beginning. I only recorded the alcoholic because those calls were so frequent.

Angela looks up at the ceiling for a moment. "If I told one woman that it does get better, that she can get out of a bad situation, turn her life around, and make it better for herself. If I told one woman that and it helped that one woman, then I'd feel like an inspiration."

"OK, well, you are because you helped me." She waves her hand at me dismissively. "No, really, I mean it. I've thought about you so much since we talked on the phone. You've been through a lot and yet joy just emanates from you. I've been molested and beaten and I was almost raped and almost abducted during my life, but living with an abusive man is the scariest thing. I think that you have been to hell and back."

"I know."

"I'm happy and joyous too and a bit on the cuckoo bird side. But I'll admit that I'm seeing there's a lot of pain underneath that. Hearing all these stories is making me face my own story. And I haven't even really told my story yet."

"Yours is deep," Angela says.

"So is yours. And to have been through all that you have and to be where you're at now is an inspiration."

"The thing is that I didn't even know the situation was so bad until I was out of it." She looks at her hands for a moment. "I can remember back in my late teens, early twenties, when I used to think it took a certain type of woman to put up with abuse. I used to think that I'd never let anyone do that to me. But you never know until you've lived through it. I never thought I'd stay for so long."

"How did you get out?" I know I'm pushing, but I figure she can handle it. She looks at me sideways for a second before answering. She can tell I'm trying to get her to talk.

"Like I said, I didn't even know it was bad until I was out. I was going to court and thinking, 'Why am I in here with all of these people? This isn't me.' And one day I was sitting at home and I was reading through all my court papers and it clicked. They weren't talking about anybody else. This was my life." She looks off for a moment. "But I overcame it. I'm not in that place anymore and I'm so grateful not to be."

"Were you scared for your life? When you were out?"

"Oh yes. I locked all the doors to my little apartment and relocked them again and again. But after a while I decided that I wasn't going to live in fear for the rest of my life."

"Do you like yourself?"

"I love myself. I'm a cute, fat black girl." We both lean forward in a heap of giggles. "And I'll be honest with you. I'd rather be by myself for the rest of my life than to go through that ever again." I think about my phone conversations with her. She told me about how her husband used to beat her—landed her in the hospital more than a few times.

"Were there police reports?"

"Oh yeah."

"Did they help you, the police?"

"Um. I didn't find them helpful, no. And I think most people are aware that law enforcement officers are some of the biggest domestic abusers. And then when you're married to a law enforcement officer, it doesn't help," she says quietly and covers her discomfort with a big laugh. I'm in shock.

"You mean your ex was a police officer?" I ask her as new understanding dawns.

"That's why I didn't want to answer the question."

"I had no idea." I'm shocked. "Talk about having to hide it." She nods. I think about how true it is that things aren't always as they seem. I bet her husband acted like he was the nicest guy in the world when he was out in public just like my dad did.

"It's scary when nobody knows about it. When you don't tell your family or your friends."

"Did you have to hide anything, like bruises?"

"Oh yeah. You find yourself lying a lot. You can be an honest person and find yourself lying a lot."

"Did you pull the whole 'I fell down the stairs' bit?"

"I've slipped on a rug, no more throw rugs in the house . . ." She waves her hands and laughs it off. "'Gosh, I was so clumsy.' You find yourself lying a lot. And I think that's what makes you realize it. But you wake up one day and start building yourself back up—hopefully."

"How did you build yourself back up?"

"I have to say it was God," Angela says and shrugs her shoulders. "My mother always told me that God would not put more on me than I could bear. And at the time I thought, 'Well, God, it's about that time. I don't know how much more of this I can take.' And just when I thought I couldn't bear any more and it seemed like I was at the end, the situation got better and kept getting better. And I think sometimes you have to live a little and hurt a little before you realize what your purpose is."

"And what is your purpose?"

"It's to just be a good person. I know for sure that my purpose is not to be abused and hurt and betrayed and treated like dirt. This was five years ago, and I've worked on myself a lot. I just had this house built."

"Hallelujah. I'm so proud of you."

"Thank you. I am too. A lot of people would say that they were proud of me if they knew what happened, but it took me a long time to feel proud of myself. Now I'm proud of what I did, and I'm still going. When you have somebody telling you you're never going to amount to anything or you're never going to be anything without him, you can start to believe it and wonder if you'll ever be OK. Now I know that I can do anything I want to do. I didn't think that before, but I know that now."

"Do you have any parting wisdom to share with women?"

"Keep believing in yourself. Women are great."

Angela and I share a big, long hug before my crew and I get back on the road. I squeeze myself, hoping that some of Angela Shelton rubbed off on me.

1979

"Swim to me, honey," my father said as the shark's fin went by in the distance. Before I could get to him, a wave came and took me under instead. I hit the bottom and drank in salt water and sand. I couldn't tell which way was up and thought I was drowning. I wondered if everyone would miss me. I thought about my mother.

A wave finally pushed me to the surface and Steve ran over to pull me out. I rolled over and threw up salt water. My stepmother yelled at my dad for having me out too far. I wanted to cover for him and take the blame, but I was still trying to breathe.

Day 33 of the search
Somewhere in North Carolina

"You do realize that Father's Day is two weeks away, don't you?" Gallo asks. He can be so annoying sometimes. I'm driving and staring straight ahead into the rain. I squeeze the wheel harder and ignore him. The last thing I want to think about right now is my dad. I have other Angela Sheltons to meet, but my crew and I will stop to see my mom and her family first for a break. They never know when I'll show up here or whom I'll have with me. I grin to myself that this time I'm showing up with a camera crew and a 33-foot motor home.

Day 34 of the search
Somewhere in North Carolina

"What do you think about me going to see my dad on Father's Day?" I ask my grandmother. She is sitting on the far side of a porch swing next to my mother and my aunt Susie. My grandmother, whom I've called Gran since I was little, looks me up and down and grins.

"That would be very interesting. Is that what you plan to do?"

"Yes, there's an Angela Shelton who lives in his town."

"There is, is there?" Gran looks like she'd like to be a part of that trip. I picture her carrying a shotgun like she intended to do when she came to the courthouse for my father's hearing.

"And she tracks sexual predators too."

"You don't say. Isn't that interesting. Think he'll talk to you?"

"I'd love to be a fly on the wall," my aunt says from the other side of the swing. My mother nods. I have coerced them all to sit out here and talk to me about my movie as well as put my crew and me up for a few days while we're passing through.

"I think it's good that you're willing to look at your past, sweetheart," my mom says. "It took you writing a movie about our life for me to see what I was doing in my life." She's right. After *Tumbleweeds* was made into a movie, she finally saw herself on the big screen. It inspired her to leave her fifth husband. "This has to help somebody somehow. You didn't ask me, but I think you're fulfilling your mission for this lifetime." I want to ask what she thinks my mission is, but that might get too esoteric for Gran and Susie, so I ask something else.

"What do you think about what happened to me as a kid?" I look at all three of them. They rock on the swing for a moment, staring at me.

"I think it was terrible," Gran says. "No child should ever have to go through anything like that." I wonder if now is the time to bring up the fact that she beat my mother.

"Is there anything you would have done differently?"

"I would have never let you go live with your father in the first place," my mother says. She looks irritated. I figure she's thinking about her family saying she was unfit as a mother and that I should live with my dad and his new family because they went to church. Maybe she's irritated at herself for not fighting harder against her family.

"I think the decision was that everyone thought at the time that they were looking out for your best interest," my aunt shares. "You were most important at the time."

"Would you have still thought that now?"

"Now that I know what your father did to you? No. Who would have ever thought that though? He was the deceiver. He made a perfect picture."

"He was with the wife, the dog, and the two kids," I add.

"Yes. He knew how to appear as though he had it all together. That he was part of the perfect American family."

"Was he weird when he was married to you, Mom?"

"He started talking to a Christmas tree like it was a person one time. That was about it. And there was that time—I've told you this before—when he took off his clothes in front of that woman we were friends with. We hung out with this couple, and he went over to their house when her husband wasn't home and took off all his clothes and stood in her living room. She called me about it, and she and her husband never hung out with us after that."

"Gross."

"And he was at that job with those delinquent boys, the juvenile home. He was a counselor or something. But back then

I was so dumb, Angela. I didn't think to question anything. I wouldn't have thought anything about it. He did go to the doctor and was diagnosed as a paranoid schizophrenic. The doctor wanted to give him electric shock therapy. I didn't know anything about health at the time or eating well or anything, but I did know that electric shock therapy didn't make any sense, so I did not consent to it."

"What happened? Why was he even seen by the doctor?"

"His parents took him to the doctor because he was talking to the Christmas tree like he was on the radio. You know, he used to be on the radio."

"I remember you telling me."

"He was very good. That's when I met him. He always wanted to be on the radio. But the doctor checked him out and wanted to give him that shock treatment, and I thought it was so strange. After that his parents gave us the money to move away, so we got that trailer. That was where we were living when you were born."

"Born in a trailer."

"That's right. Well, honey, at least you always have something to write about, right? You have so many stories, you could write for your whole life." My mother has a strange way of always looking on the bright side.

My grandmother, the queen of segues, leans in. "Your daddy's mother tried to blame it all on those magazines. Remember that?" She looks over at my mother. "When we went there after the hearing, she said if it hadn't been for those magazines that what's his name had . . . the boy—what was the boy's name?"

"You mean my brother, Steve?"

"That ain't your brother."

"Gran, that is my brother. I consider him my brother."

"Well, your dad's mother said if it weren't for them magazines he had, none of this would have happened. And I told her that boy didn't have those magazines—it was your daddy who had them. And she wasn't hearing any of it. She just wasn't having it."

"They've always protected him," my mother says. Gran nods.

"There's some funny business going on in that family."

"I know. I think that it all goes back to her father, to my dad's grandpa," I theorize. Gran and my mother nod as they swing on the swing.

"Your great-granddaddy? Interesting."

"I think something happened to my grandmother, my dad's mom. I really do. And I've always suspected it was something with her dad. I don't know, but there's something weird there. And my grandmother used to leave my dad with her father when my dad was little. She had her father babysit her son. I wouldn't be surprised if that was my dad's first introduction to abuse. It's just my own theory, but I suspect that his grandfather sexually abused him and his grandfather was the same man who abused my grandmother too. And she's been covering up for both of them all these years. That's just my take on the whole thing. She is just too weird and has too many obsessive behaviors to not have it linked to some kind of abuse."

"I guess we'll never know because she won't talk. Remember when we went there and she ran us out of the house?" Gran asks, rolling her eyes. She is talking about when I was 18 and I came back to town to pick up all the court papers from the hearing. I went with Gran and my mother to deliver them to my dad's parents. But they ran us off.

"I remember that. Do you remember the trial?"

"Some of it," Gran says. "I remember our lawyer rushing out after you were on the stand and saying, 'Boy, she really fixed her daddy.'" I've heard that story before. It makes me remember that day. I can see the witness stand and the clock on the wall in the back of the courtroom. "It was you who told about him ejaculating or whatever. You told on him. I loved that."

"It was a big deal, that trial," my mother says. "Every lawyer in the whole county was there. There were five of them." We all laugh.

"And your daddy said that it was their way of life, their sex training," Gran says with distain.

"Sex education in the home was his excuse," my mother adds.

"No telling what will come up with you going there," Gran says and looks off down the road.

"He'll just deny it. He always has," my mother says.

"Weren't you molested too, Mom?" I love to shake up the family. Maybe it's my deep-seated need to stick up for my mother because of all the times the other family members tore her down.

"Yes. My grandfather molested me," my mother says with no expression.

My grandmother jerks her head toward my mom as quick as a hornet. "What? My dad?" My mom nods.

"You never know what will show up when you get to talking, do you?" Gran says and then stares off down the road.

"Did he ever do anything to you, Gran?"

Gran looks at me quickly and snaps "No" very frankly.

I don't believe her. "All I can say is that everyone knows someone who was sexually abused, whether you know it or not. At least that's what I'm finding."

"If they tell it," my aunt Susie adds. I nod, already knowing the story she isn't sharing. I wait for her to pipe up with her own past, but she just sits there and looks at my mom and my grandmother and then back at me.

"Everybody's got a skeleton in the closet," Gran says. I feel like bringing up the fact that she beat the living hell out of my mother when she was growing up, but I don't.

"What do you think about me going around meeting every Angela Shelton?" I segue.

Gran thinks for a moment and then leans forward and says, "If there was that many Angela Sheltons that were treated like that, just think how many more women who are not Angela Sheltons who have been treated the same way."

Dream Journal—June 5, 2001
I dreamed a bird flew into my window and was trying to tell me something but I couldn't hear it because of the rain

Day 35 of the search
Somewhere in North Carolina

"There's a lot of people out there hurting," my uncle Toby says as we film him sitting on his back porch. "It's good for you to bring it all up. I mean just the other day there was a story about some poor old feller who was being beaten up by his wife, so it ain't just women who are going through it." He spits tobacco juice into his paper cup. "I just wish I was going with you, honey."

"Where?"

"To your daddy's."

"Oh. Why? What would you do?"

"It's not what I'd do; it's what your daddy would do." He looks straight at me like he's looking down the barrel of one of his shotguns. "You might have to protect him. I'd get him riled up so bad that he'd take a swing at me, and it'd be the worst mistake of his life. 'Cause, honey, you can't go around roughing people up, especially on their own property," he says like he has experience. "But if he takes a swing at me first, I have every right in the world to defend myself, and I'm telling you, I'd do it."

I half wish that I could take my uncle with me just to be able to see that. But I don't want to turn this into a witch hunt. I just want to see my dad. Maybe I'll get my dad back. Maybe he'll admit he was wrong, say he's sorry, and we can start a new relationship.

We go back into the house. My mom has all the picture books laid out on the floor. That's the main pastime when I visit my grandmother's house: looking through pictures from the past. I sit next to my mom on the floor. She holds the book of photos from when I was a baby. There are pictures of her and my dad too. It is weird to see him. I cut his head and body out of all the pictures I have. There is one image of my mom and dad sitting in the car after they got married. There are the usual decorations on the car, but instead of saying "Just Married" it says "Sorry" on the side of the door.

"Who wrote that?" I ask my mom.

"I have no idea. Probably one of his friends as a joke." She looks at the photo for a moment and then over at me. "It's fitting though, isn't it? I am sorry, sweetheart. I'm sorry I let you go live with him. I'm sorry I wasn't there to protect you."

"You didn't know. And everyone was telling you to let me go. And he hid it so well."

"I know, but I should have known better. I should have fought my family."

I look at my grandmother in the kitchen. My mom was beaten so badly as a child and a teen that she swore to be the exact opposite of her mother. Once my mother regained custody of me, there were not many rules in our house. I never had a curfew. She never laid a hand on me either. She treated me like an adult and let me do what I wanted. And because of that, I had no desire to sneak out of the house like my friends did because I could walk out the front door if I cared to. I am grateful my mother chose not to become like her mom. Looking at her past and where she came from, I understand so much more.

"You are a good mom, Mama. You are." Her eyes well up with tears as she turns the page and reaches over to squeeze my hand.

I wouldn't change anything. If I hadn't been through everything I had, I wouldn't be sitting here. And I wouldn't be making this movie.

My mom turns the page to a whole set of pictures of me. "You did get your father's looks, honey. At least he was good for something."

1981

I stared at the clock in the back of the courtroom like the social workers, Ms. Ford and Ms. Lemons, told me to do. "Keep focused on the clock. It will keep you from thinking about your dad. Just look at the clock and answer the questions."

I stayed focused on the clock. I couldn't see what time it was because my eyes were drawn back toward my dad. He was sitting at a long table to my left next to my stepmother and their lawyer. He looked right at me and shook his head from side to side, disappointed. I was in trouble and I knew I should shut up. I felt a creepy crawly feeling move up my back. I kicked the inside of

PART I

the witness stand with my patent leather shoes again and again as my father's lawyer yelled at me.

"It was lotion that you saw. The white stuff on your hands, it was lotion, wasn't it, Angie?" I figured that this guy knew all about the massages we had to give my dad and stepmom. That's when we used the lotion. But it was pink, the kind that I remember. It wasn't white. I didn't know what I was supposed to say. I wished this man would stop yelling at me. He was making me nervous and was twisting my words around. I felt like I was stupid. I kicked the inside of the witness box and wondered when my father was going to jump up and interrupt him. I wondered when my dad was going to say he was sorry and come lift me out of that witness stand. I stared at the clock and nothing happened. My dad didn't come to rescue me. He didn't yell out across the courtroom that he was sorry. He just sat there.

"Tell the court that it was the lotion that you saw."

I looked at the clock. What time was it? I thought about the social workers coming to get my stepsister and me out of school. I thought about my old room and wondered if I'd ever see it again.

"Wasn't it lotion?" the lawyer repeated and started approaching me. He was really mean. I didn't like him at all. He had been yelling at me for what seemed like forever.

"No," I said. "It wasn't lotion. It was white stuff that squirted out of the top of daddy's thingy."

Silence. The lawyer stopped. Everyone stopped. I looked at my dad and then remembered that I wasn't supposed to. I looked down at my shoe. I tapped it on the inside of the witness stand and then looked back at the clock.

"No further questions."

Day 36 of the search
Angela Shelton in Tennessee

"Does Angela Shelton work here?" I ask into the Taco Bell drive-through speaker. Luckily the RV fits through the drive-through, so I order an Angela Shelton.

"She sure does, hold on," the speaker answers back. I wonder if I should tack a burrito or two onto my Angela Shelton order. After a second the speaker garbles back.

"Hello?"

"Is this Angela Shelton?" I ask in my Southern accent.

"It sure is," Angela answers back with her Southern drawl.

"This is Angie Shelton." Silence. "I found you," I tease, but still get silence. "Hello? Can I pull up to the window?"

After a long pause Angela answers tightly, "Pull on up." The Angela Shelton in Tennessee is a Caucasian blonde Southern woman who looks like she could break you in half. She manages a Taco Bell, and she is not too pleased to see me. She and I spent about an hour on the phone when I first called all the Angelas. She was one of the many who thought it was a joke. But I guess she thought that it was safe to talk to a stranger and needed to because she told me all about her life. But when I called her back to tell her I was on my way, she would not call me back. I left message after message with dates and times that I'd be here, but she avoided me.

I ask if she can talk, and she tells me I'll have to wait until her break, so my crew and I pull into the parking lot and wait until she can take a moment off. I loiter outside the doorway, reminding her of my presence. Finally she takes her apron off and motions for me to come inside. I know a lot of her story from our phone conversation. I know that she's pregnant.

"This is exciting," I say and motion to her protruding belly. "Are you still with the father?"

"No. He's nothing important." She doesn't blink an eye. I wonder how the father of a child could not be important, but then again my father was more of a sperm donor than a father. I bring her up-to-date about all the Angela Sheltons I've met so far and where I am at in my journey.

"They're all awesome women, and some have really been through the wringer like the rest of us, but they have really built themselves back up."

"That's good." She seems completely disinterested.

"So who would you say you are?"

"I'm another Angela Shelton, I guess." I watch the first smile I've seen appear on her face. "We're everywhere."

"What do you think about what I'm doing?"

"It's wild, especially when it comes to hitting this close to home, you know what I mean?" I nod. I know.

"Do you want to tell me your story?"

"No. The world doesn't need to know all about that."

"Do you like yourself?"

"I guess, yeah." She looks around the room nervously.

"What makes you angry?"

"People. People in general make me angry. People tear my nerves up. They like to stir the pot."

"What about?"

"I am not going to discuss what happened." She can tell I'm trying to lead her somewhere.

"Why not?"

"Because it's nobody's business. And it's just . . ." She pauses and looks back over at the counter. I figure she's waiting for her break to be over so she can tell me to buzz off. "Men can be cruel." She turns back to me. "They really can. They can be extremely cruel. And then, of course, it's always the woman's fault. So I've learned to chalk it up to 'OK, I did it, OK, go on' so it will be over."

"Doesn't that hurt you in the long run?"

"It hurts then, but a person can get over anything if she tries." She looks like she's still hurting. I want to hug her, but I'm afraid she'll punch me.

"What's your secret? Are you over it yet?"

"I'm strong willed. I ain't going to let nobody bring me down no more. That's my secret."

"Is there anything you would tell women who are going through turmoil? Any advice?" She cocks her head to one side and thinks about it.

"No relationship is worth losing the most important thing in your life," she says after a moment. "None, not one that I can think of. Nothing is more important to me than my children. They are my life. And I wouldn't let anybody get me down to the point of actually wanting to hurt somebody, because eventually a person will. You really will. I would hurt somebody over my younguns. Simple."

I believe her. I think of my mother telling me how my grandmother packed a pistol in her purse when they went to the family court hearing. I wonder what they would have done had they known about the abuse earlier. During the court hearing my mother and my grandmother bonded like they hadn't ever before. They had something to fight for together instead of my grandmother simply beating my mom. I think about my mother and how there was a time when I resented her for leaving me with my dad. I hated that she believed his act. The only woman who knew what was going on was my stepmother. She's the one I've been mad at all these years, not my real mother. But all of them could have been better mothers. It's like the wounded children are having children and are continuing the cycle over and over again. I have a fantasy while watching the face of this cranky Angela Shelton of all mothers protecting their children. I recall how the Angela in northern California said she was raising her boys to respect others and not victimize anyone. The Angela in Tennessee looks at me sideways. I think about wounded mothers and how it will be an interesting world when the victims heal and break the cycle. I glance down at Angela Shelton's belly and hope that happens soon.

1990

When I was 18 I got a letter out of the blue from my long-lost stepsister. I was living in California with my mom and her fifth husband. I'm not sure how Lisa found me, but her letter got into my hands. I opened it, unsure of the return address. The first line said, "I don't know if you'll remember me but I was your sister once for five years . . ." That's when my tears started. For years I had thought that my stepsister and stepbrother hated me and never wanted to see me again. I thought they blamed me for what my dad did. Their dad had told my mother that Lisa and Steve didn't want to be reminded of the past and didn't want anything to do with me. In the letter Lisa explained how her dad told her and Steve that my mom said the same thing about me not wanting to see them. He successfully separated us, thinking it was for our own good. I thought he was a jerk. My stepsister wrote that she was getting married and wanted to know if I would come to her wedding. We could see each other for the first time in 10 years. My tears didn't stop until I was at the end of the letter, when I was rushing for the phone. She had included her number at the end of the letter.

I dialed and recognized her voice immediately. I choked back my flood of emotion and said hello. She was so excited. "Oh my God, Angie!"

We cried for a while. "I missed you so much. I thought you hated me."

"No way, are you crazy? I love you. I only found out that my dad had lied about the whole thing recently. He said he wanted to protect us. Stupid."

"Yeah, stupid. What happened to you and Steve? Where did you go? I never knew. I was just sent to my mom's."

"We both went to live with Dad."

"Was it great?"

"It was all right, not great—better than your dad though."

"I bet."

"My dad isn't a peach. I wouldn't say it was easy for Steve and me. How's your mother? I always loved your mother."

"I know, me too. She's great, but she's a nut. She's married to her fifth husband now. Do you talk to your mother still?"

"Yeah. She's married to a new guy. I still talk to her, but you know, it's strange."

"I'm sorry."

"For what?"

"For what my dad did. I'm really sorry. I've thought about it so much over the years. I can't believe he's my father. I always wanted to know what he did to you."

"It's not your fault."

"I know, but . . . I'd like to know. All I remember is your mother sending you into the room with him. I can see it clearly— on that waterbed."

"God, I hate waterbeds. I don't know if I can go into that. I don't want to talk about that."

"I know. But . . . Did he rape you in there? I mean you don't have to say. I just want to know. I'm sorry."

"No. He tried. But it wouldn't fit. You know, his . . . He wouldn't fit so he used other things."

"What other things?"

"Um. Crayons. And Magic Markers."

"Oh my God." I want to claw at something. I don't know what to do.

"He told me that he had to use those to work up to his thing. That it was the way to work me in."

I feel anger like I've never felt before. I don't know what to do. I make a joke. "So that's why you never wanted to color with me."

Lisa bursts out laughing. I laugh with her to hide my rage. "That's why you were always coloring and I was not. Oh my God, can we talk about something else?"

"Yes. But have you read *The Courage to Heal?*"

"No."

"I read it a few years ago when I was 16. It had a big impact on me. You should read it, if you want."

"Maybe I will one day, but I don't think I want to talk about that part of my life. I didn't want to lose you though."

"I'm really excited to see you again soon. I can't tell you how happy I am that you wrote me, that you found me."

"I'm glad you remembered me."

"Are you crazy? You're my sister."

"Do you think you can come to my wedding?"

I knew my mother would say yes before I even asked her. We packed up the car and drove in the direction we'd come from years before when she left her fourth husband. Driving away from California and toward the mountains of North Carolina was bittersweet for both of us.

"I'd love to move back here one day," my mother dreamed as we turned the corner onto the Blue Ridge Parkway.

"I love it," I agreed. "But it gives me the creeps." A memory hit me of the A-frame house I lived in with my dad before my stepsister and I were removed from the house. That house was so dark and looming. The green shag carpet tried to keep it cheerful looking but failed. It made me want to puke. "I want to go to the courthouse while we're there. I want to get those court papers. I'm 18 now, so I can."

My mother turned to me while she drove and looked me up and down. I could see her from my peripheral vision, but I looked straight ahead. "All right. We can do that. What are you going to do with them? You think you can go after him now?"

"I don't know. I just want them."

"I'm so sorry, honey, for not getting that transcript back then." She looked toward me again. She had apologized for this numerous times before. I was sick of hearing it. There had been a transcript of the entire day in court. It was expensive back then to order a copy and none of my family members did. My mom hadn't seen a reason to have it. I wanted a copy after I read *The Courage to Heal*. At least then I would know what my stepbrother and stepsister had said. We hadn't been allowed to be in the courtroom at the same time when we told our story on the stand. I wanted to know what my father had done to my stepsister or if she even told. I had called the courthouse when I was 16, but the court employee told me that there had been a big flood and all the cases from that corridor had been destroyed. No one had ordered a copy.

"You can't get a transcript. They drowned," the person who was on the phone had said. She was trying to be funny. I didn't laugh.

"Is there anything else I can get?"

"There are all the other court records from those proceedings, but no transcript. But you have to be 18 to order a copy," the person warned me.

I was going to go get those papers now. My mother looked over at me. She could tell I was lost in thought. I was floating around in the past. "We can go to the courthouse after the wedding if you want."

"I want to."

We pulled up to the church that my sister was getting married in. I was nervous to see everyone again. The front windows resembled those on the A-frame house. The hair on the back of my neck stood up, but I ignored it because I had made it to my long-lost sister's wedding. She was as beautiful at 22 as she had been at 10 years old. She still looked like a child. She looked just like my sister. I didn't know what to say; neither one of us did. We just smiled at each other and hugged. I saw Steve briefly over her shoulder. He nodded at me from afar and then avoided me. My stepmother came over. That was awkward. She had sent me greeting cards for years and I had never responded.

"Angie, it's so good to see you. It's been so long. You look just the same."

I wanted to scream. Do people really just ignore things? Do families just continue on with their weddings and births and never address core issues? My stepmother leaned in to hug me and I let her. I was as bad as everyone else. She and my mom nodded to each other. My mom didn't say anything either. Another woman would have hauled off and slugged her, but my mother just grinned her perfect Southern charmer grin. This was my sister's day. We didn't want to make a scene. My stepmother, or ex-stepmother, introduced us to her new husband. He looked just like my dad.

My mom and I whispered to each other about it as we found our seats in the church. I hated being there. I felt dirty. I felt like eyes were leaning forward to get a look at the long-lost stepsister, the daughter of the devil himself. I wanted to run screaming for the doors, but I sat there and watched my sister marry a creep. I ran the tip of my shoe on the inside of the pew like I had tapped my foot on the inside of the witness stand when I was 8.

My sister rode off toward her honeymoon, and my mother and I drove to the courthouse in the adjacent county. Just pulling up in front made me want to hurl. I felt like my feet were not touching the concrete as we walked to the entrance. I told the lady at the counter why I was there and she looked nervous. I had to show my ID and prove that I was 18 before the court employee gave me copies of the records on my own family court hearing. I was so mad at the bureaucracy; I almost saw red. She reminded me that there was no transcript.

"I know. There was a flood. I'll take copies of whatever is left from that hearing." She nodded and moved down the hallway. She came back with a big folder on my family.

"And you're Miss—"

"Shelton. I changed my name. I didn't want my father's name. He's a child molester."

The lady looked up at me and then quickly went around the corner into an office and talked to someone for a moment. She came back to her desk and started making copies. After a while she handed me a huge stack of legal-size court papers. I had to sign for them. My mother was there for support. She nodded to me. I felt like I wasn't in my body as I took the papers from the court lady. The judge came out of his chambers right then and came walking toward me. Apparently he had been told that I was there and that I was picking up the papers. He came over and put his hand on my shoulder. He gave me the willies.

"I'm not sure why you're picking these up or what you have in mind, young lady," the family court judge said. "But I just want to tell you that people do change."

I wondered if family court was some big club for creeps. I wondered if that was the reason nothing ever happened to my dad. I walked away from that judge as quickly as I could, holding on tightly to the court documents. I wondered if there really had been a flood in the corridors.

Dream Journal—June 7, 2001
   I dreamed that a man was chasing me down a series of dark hallways. I couldn't see who he was; I could only hear his footsteps. I was running looking down each corridor that I passed I could hear distant whispering I was searching for the dead body I was supposed to bring out into the light.

Day 38 of the search
My brother's house in South Carolina

I have a lump in my throat the size of Texas. We only have about an hour and a half before we arrive at my stepbrother's house and I am beside myself. If I feel like this going to see

Steve, then seeing my dad will either be a piece of cake or I'll fall over dead from the anxiety.

"How do you feel?" Gallo asks with the camera pointed at me. I don't want to talk. If I say anything I'll start to cry.

"I'm nervous," I whisper through clenched teeth. "I don't really know how I feel. I haven't talked to Steve since I was 8 years old. Last time I talked to him at all was when I was 18, 10 years ago. I came down here like the black sheep of the family and picked up all the court papers. I went to my sister's wedding, but he completely avoided me there. And now I'm going to his house, and I don't really know how I feel." I really want to drop my crew off at a local store and go see my stepbrother by myself. I feel sick to my stomach. I can hardly focus on the road because of the well of tears collecting in my eyes.

I turn the corner to Steve's house and pull up to the curb a few houses down. Lisa was the one who called me and told me that Steve wanted to talk to me. When she told him that she was going to talk to me for my documentary, she told him that she knew he wouldn't and had already told me no on his behalf. But he surprised her when he said that might not be the case. She called me at my aunt Susie's house after I was done banging the gong of the past. She gave me his phone number, and I called him immediately, not giving myself any time to reconsider. We spoke briefly and he gave me directions to his house.

I'm out the door before Giovanni has me wired and Gallo has a new tape loaded in the camera. They jump down and stop me from walking down the sidewalk. I'm antsy and want to get this over with. I make the whole crew wait across the street while I go up to the house alone. I knock. Steve answers. He looks like the grown-up version of the boy I lived with when I was little. We stand there looking at each other. Neither one of us knows what to do next. Steve steps outside. I point to the crew across the street and laugh. After a moment of awkwardness, we hug each other.

"What are they doing all the way over there?"

"I didn't want them coming up here with me. I don't know, I felt weird about it."

"You better tell them to come on if you're shooting a movie," Steve directs me. I wave the crew up, and they make their way across the street and up the stairs into the house. We all get situated and find a place to talk. Giovanni wires Steve, and Gallo starts filming while Chantal takes notes and Sylvia stands waiting as Gallo's assistant. There is no prep time. There is no time to talk about what we're going to discuss or where this will lead. I just begin.

"What do you think about all this?"

"Well, it's good to see you," Steve says. "I was hoping you'd come visit me sometime. And you can come again without the cameras if you want."

"OK. Thank you so much for talking to me." He grins but seems slightly nervous. "And I have to ask, might as well throw it out there . . ." Steve adjusts himself in his chair as if preparing for something hard.

"Lay it on me," he sighs.

"I really want to know what my dad did to you. I mean I have my theories." Steve takes a deep breath.

"Honestly, I don't remember." I feel like he's avoiding me, but he continues. "Everything that happened occurred right out in the open, as you know. And I think you, Lisa, and my dad think things happened with me and your dad when you weren't around, and all I can say is that I don't remember." I nod, remembering the times that Steve had to go into my dad's bedroom alone. Perhaps it's possible to repress memories. "I wasn't his focus," Steve says. We look at each other, both thinking about our sister. "I do remember him showing my mother off to me." That memory bounces into focus in my mind. I can see it happening as he describes it. "There I was right in the middle of the Oedipal stage and my mother's husband was showing my mother off to me. Talk about conflict," he says in his overly queenly way. I can see my stepmother laid out naked on the waterbed and my dad trying to get Steve to put his thing in her. It was sexual education, my dad asserted. He was teaching us how it was done. "And there were many things other than the molestation that happened to me later," Steve says. "I had the molested child syndrome. I went through hypersexuality and low self-esteem. I slept with my first guy at 16. He was an older man, and I could not believe that he wanted to have sex with me. It just blew me away. And now I look back at pictures of myself and I was beautiful." I nod in agreement. He was beautiful.

It makes me think of all the relationships I've been in simply so I wasn't alone. It's amazing how we don't see ourselves. I think back to when I was modeling and was with verbally abusive men. I didn't even see that I was the prize. I was simply happy that someone wanted to be with me, just like Steve said. Then I realize something for the first time. I am the one who became a model. My father used to bring out all the porno magazines and have my beautiful sister pose for him, and yet I was the one who grew up to be the model. I've never thought about that before. That's another level of trying to be seen. I have a flash of how my whole life, losing my virginity, my relationships, my work, everything has been affected by the beliefs that were set in place when I was little. I believed I wasn't good enough, that I was ugly, dirty, and ruined, and I pulled experiences to me to confirm that belief. I am suddenly so grateful that my mother won custody of me when she did. She was the opposite of my father. She always told me that I was talented and lovely and could accomplish anything.

"Do you think that all the things that happened to you were products of being molested?" I ask my brother as I am flooded with these realizations.

"No. I think it's impossible to have an ABC list of where everything came from, but if I wanted to have a pity party I could say I was dealt a lousy hand. I was molested early and then I wound up being gay in one of the most conservative areas of the country. And I've had so many people ask me if I was gay because I was molested. Short answer no, long answer yes." I want to point out to him that he just said he was molested but claimed to not remember anything. I wonder what he remembers deep within his subconscious. I don't rewind though. I keep moving forward, amazed that I'm even sitting here having this conversation.

"I've been through the same thing," I confess. "My dad used to make us jerk him off in there." Steve shakes his head uncomfortably. "I was taught that I had to please a man and how to do it. And I was the one nobody wanted. You wanted Lisa more than me too, and so did my dad. You know what he did to Lisa, right?"

"No," Steve says quietly and holds up his hand before I can tell him any more. "And I don't want to know. If she wants me to know, she can tell me herself."

"There was a lot, but OK." I stop before he stops me. "My dad was always sexual. You remember how he used to make us all get naked, right?"

"Oh yeah. And the Polaroids," he adds.

"Polaroids?" I don't remember any Polaroids.

"You don't remember that?" Steve asks. He seems as amazed as I was when he said he didn't remember being alone with my dad. "He used to take Polaroids of us doing stuff to Mom," he tells me. It's now my turn to not remember. It's as if that memory isn't accessible in my brain, like it was erased. I search for it, but nothing comes up. My mind is blank.

"Oh my God," I say, genuinely shocked.

"That's classic pedophilia," Steve points out. "I read up on all of it later in life. Molesters keep mementos like that."

"Ewww." Steve nods.

"I know. I kept telling the attorney. I said, 'Look, we don't have to go to court. There's a whole picture book full of this stuff. All you have to do is get a search warrant and go get the pictures. They're all there.' But I'm sure they were destroyed before the hearing."

"That's sick." I'm ashamed of my father. "And then all the things he did to Lisa." I don't go into detail because of the look on Steve's face. "I went through such guilt," I admit. "Because he's my dad. I went through major, major guilt and still do." Steve looks at the floor.

"The guilt that I went through—and I think this is the guilt that most molested children go through—was that there was a part of me that enjoyed it. It was exciting. Because there's a natural inclination to be sexual. But it was too early. You don't give a 5-year-old beer in their bottle, and you don't give a child sexuality. They're not ready to handle it. It took me awhile to realize that sexuality is OK. We were just exposed way too early and by the wrong people. Some of the things I've done have been the hardest for me to deal with," he confesses. I know what he's talking about. I'm thankful that he brings it up first.

. "What you did to Lisa and me was only learned behavior." He looks at me and then at the floor again.

"That is by far the most horrible part for me. That is the thing that I've had the most difficult time dealing with. That is my nightmare, and I think that's probably one of the reasons I've avoided you." He looks at me apologetically and then down at his hands. I watch tears well up in his eyes.

"I forgive you," I say quietly and unexpectedly. Steve is taken aback as he looks up at me.

"Thank you." He looks directly at me. Then he smiles, grateful. "I'm working on forgiving myself."

"What you did was learned behavior."

"And the mental, logical side of my mind knows that. But the emotional side is trying to catch up." I understand completely. I hope that I can catch up to him and all the Angela Sheltons. I'm the one who feels behind.

"What do you think about what I'm doing?" I ask my step-brother to try to get some encouragement.

"God's honest truth?" I nod. "I think that you're looking for something, and I hope that you find what you're looking for. That's the only reason I'm here. That's the only reason I agreed to do this." I feel the tears well up in my eyes. "When Lisa called me and told me you were doing this, I'll admit I was vehemently opposed to it. But then I thought that by staying silent I was contributing to the culture of silence that goes along with this." He leans forward and takes my hands. "I want it to be OK for you. That's why I'm here. That's why I agreed to do this." He looks lovingly into my eyes, and I believe him. I don't know what to do. I appear to have a brother again.

"It is OK for me—it's just hard." I wish I didn't have a crew around me. I want to roll into a ball and have a good cry.

"It's hard, I know it is," Steve says. He knows I need time.

"I have this weird sense of protecting him," I admit in all honesty. "That's my dad." I miss my dad. I wish I had a dad.

"I know exactly how you feel. Because they're our parents, they are the only ones we can have and we love them because of that."

"I'm so sorry for what he did," I say suddenly. I barely get it out before crying.

"It's not your fault."

"I know."

"It had nothing to do with you."

"I know. But he's my dad. I feel like I have a vaccine. Like I'm the only one carrying his blood. I'm his only child. I feel like I'm on a crusade to fix all the things that he ever did to kids, you know? You have to have the disease to create the vaccine."

"You can't fix it all," Steve warns.

"I know. But I can try. I will try."

"You have to allow yourself to move on," my brother warns. I nod like I know, but I don't know.

"What did you do to move on?"

"I try to be the best person I can be. And my faith has helped me a lot. There comes a time in your life that you are no longer merely the product of your parents. There comes a time in your life that you become your own person, and yes, bad things may have happened to you, but you decide how the rest of the story goes." I wonder how the rest of the story will go for me.

"I feel like you're my brother, not a stepbrother."

"The 'step' means nothing to me. I will always claim you as my sister."

"I claim you as my brother too."

Day 39 of the search
My sister in South Carolina

"I can't believe he agreed to talk to you," Lisa says as we walk across the parking lot. She's come to meet me on her lunch hour. She's as amazed as I am that our brother talked to me on camera. Now it's her turn.

"I hate that every time we see each other or talk on the phone that it leads to this subject," I tell her. I want to apologize beforehand because I have every intention of asking her about my dad.

"It's all right. I'll talk with you about it again for the camera as long as it's far away. I don't need to be scaring off small children." I grimace. Lisa has always thought of herself as ugly. It's another thing my dad can take credit for. He so nicely contributed to her low self-esteem and poor self-image. I stare at her. She really is so beautiful. I wish she could see herself. "So how was Steve?" she asks.

"He said he didn't remember anything in the house in Norwood."

"What? That's where most of it happened."

"I know."

"Do you think he really blocked it out or just doesn't want to remember?"

"I don't know. I didn't push him on it."

"Maybe he has a hard time facing things because he feels guilty that he was involved," she points out. We reach a patch of grass and sit down. I nod to Gallo and Gio to keep their distance.

"Do you want to talk to me about what he did?" I ask after we sit for a moment. I might as well jump right in.

"Steve?" She surprises me. I wonder if there's more to our past than what I remember. I wasn't talking about Steve.

"No, my dad."

"Oh." She winces at the mention of him. She pinches a piece of grass out of the ground and fiddles with it between her fingers. I remember the Illinois Angela Shelton twirling a blade of grass just like that.

"Did he ever . . ." I want to ask her if my father ever penetrated her, but I can't get the words to come out of my mouth.

"He did everything you can possibly do with a child other than actual intercourse." She looks up and then goes back to her blade of grass. I remember calling her when I first received her letter when I was 18 years old. All I wanted to do was talk about what happened. I wanted details. I wanted facts. I wanted to know what my dad did to her when my stepmother led her into his room. All I remember was the waterbed and his erection. I didn't have the full picture. That was when Lisa told me everything. That was when I learned about the crayons and Magic Markers. That was the first time I felt rage toward the man I share DNA with. I hated to have her repeat it, but I wanted it on camera if I was going to go see him.

"He was actually poised to insert," she explains, reading my mind. "But then he said, 'No, not yet. We can't do it yet.'" She shakes her head and breaks a blade of grass.

"I'm sorry."

"You didn't do it."

"Yeah, but he was my dad."

"You don't have to carry around his guilt for him."

"It's amazing to me that he's not in jail," I say to the new blade of grass she twists in her hand. "He was the candy man. He owned that arcade. You know, when I went and picked up all those court papers at the courthouse . . ."

"They remember you. The whole town, they all remember it," she finishes my thought for me and shakes her head in disgust.

"You're right. I was walking by and I was like, 'Wasn't there an arcade here once?' And this man at the hardware store answered, 'Oh yeah, it was some child molester.' I thought, wow, that's my dad. They should have both gone to jail."

"They could have because at the point that the judge made a decision on custody, the next step would have been to put them in jail. But your mom and my dad didn't want to put us through a public trial, which is what it would have been. We would've had to get on a stand in front of a jury, in front of open court . . ."

"It would have been televised."

"And they made the decision that they didn't want that to happen," Lisa continues like we're the newscasters of our life.

"What would you say to someone who was going through the same thing now?" I ask, remembering the camera aimed at us from across the parking lot.

"That you can't pretend it didn't happen, but you have to be able to face it and then move on. And I don't think you ever really get past it, just like I'm overprotective of my child. But you have to reach a place where you're ready to deal with it, and if you're not ready, it's not going to do any good to talk about it." She flicks a blade of grass. I wonder if she's ready.

"What would you want to say to my dad if you were to go with me?"

"Eww. I don't know." She rips a blade of grass in two. "When you said that just now, I felt so gross. I actually would be so repulsed for him to even look at me. I wouldn't even want him to see me. It would feel like he was abusing me all over again." We sit for a moment. I'm at a loss for words. I wish I could reach into her mind and remove any images of my father and what he did and said to her.

"I'm sorry. I'm sorry for what he did."

"It's not your fault," she says to the blade of grass in her hand. "But he's my dad."

Day 40 of the search
Somewhere in Florida

I wonder if seeing my dad is going to be anything like seeing my brother. I stare at the ocean. I'm so close to where my father used to take me swimming. I'm close to the sharks. I'm headed down to Miami to see the Angela Shelton in Florida before I see my dad. Father's Day is only a few days away, and I know that I'm going to want to jet home after I see him. I have to meet the Florida Angela now if I'm going to keep her in the movie.

Day 42 of the search
Angela Shelton in Florida

"You're not going to cut me out, are you?" the Angela Shelton in Florida asks. She's an African-American woman who works in the medical field as an MRI tech. She's another caretaker like most of the Angelas. She thinks this whole idea is wild, but she's worried about being cut out. I tell her that I'm putting all the Angelas I meet in because each one means something and teaches me some kind of lesson.

"I want to cut the movie so that all the Angelas are telling one story, like it's advice to all women or one woman from all women. We just happened to be named Angela Shelton. So what would you say to women?" She grins and fiddles with her keys and looks up at the sky.

"To stay strong," she says and then she adds, "and take your rightful place." I'm not sure what that's supposed to mean. "This is something I'm working on, submitting to my husband." She makes a face as if it's hard work. I wish for a second that I had a control room somewhere where I could stop, rewind, and play back time. Did I hear that correctly? Before I can ask her about it, she continues, "But women need to unite. We need to come together first as women. Not just black women, not just white women, but women in general because that's our bond." I picture women uniting against submissiveness. I'm still stuck on her comment about submitting to her husband but decide not to press it.

"What do you think about me making this movie?"

"It's good. Women need to be heard. People all the time are listening to what the men have to say. I think it's about time they listen to the women." I almost scream out hallelujah.

"What do you think about the fact that so many of the Angela Sheltons I've spoken to have been raped, beaten, or molested?"

"Well, that hasn't happened to me," she says quickly. "But it could have. That's why it's good you're talking for all of us."

Angela has to get back to work, so I make a time to meet her later at her house and film her and her family. My crew and I drive around Miami and scope out a hotel. Then we arrive at Angela's house before she does. We meet her husband. He makes us all nervous. Maybe it's that comment about submission, or maybe it's because he's a really big, really good-looking African-American man. He's suspicious of us and eyeballs our every move as we pull out our equipment. We're relieved when Angela arrives home and stands by his side.

"How have you stayed married for so long?" I ask them both after Angela tells us they've been married for over 20 years. "Do you have any advice for young couples?"

"We play together," Angela's husband answers for both of them. "We ride bikes, walk, play tennis. We're active together. We enjoy each other's company." Angela smiles.

"Since I'm making this movie to inspire women, what do you think about women and where we're at and what we've been through and are going through?" I ask Angela's husband.

"Women? Some of them are too headstrong and independent. Some of them aren't submissive like they need to be." He looks right at me. The hair on the back of my neck stands up.

Angela grins and tucks her chin down and says, "We let men think they're in charge. They are the head, but really we are the neck, turning the head." They both laugh. I nod and remain silent. Watching them makes me think about men's power and control that has been going on for centuries and how women help their own suppression continue. We're losing light, so after I've asked the same questions I ask every Angela, my crew and I pack up and skid out of there. We are all silent as we search for the highway.

"Was he talking directly to you, Ang, with that submissive business?" Gallo jokes.

"Who knows? That was so weird." I think about the Angela Sheltons telling me to be independent and not rely on a man. Submissive means to yield oneself to the authority or will of another, like being controlled, kept silent, and having to behave. I realize as I drive onto the on-ramp that I've been submissive for the better part of my life. I was submissive with my dad in court when I was little. I was submissive in many of my past relationships. I have quieted down, stopped dancing, changed the way I dress, fixed my hairstyle, halted my creativity, and stopped singing all because these characteristics and actions made some men nervous or uncomfortable. I've been submissive.

Day 43 of the search
Traveling in Florida

There's a storm brewing far off at sea and lightning strikes in the distance. Most everyone has left the beach. We've stopped in St. Augustine on our way up the coast of Florida. One woman mumbles a warning of lightning under her breath as she rushes back to the hotel. My crew and I stay in the water. Dolphins begin appearing. The fear of lightning is not enough to keep us away from the beauty of this storm.

It's such a magical evening that I decide to let go of my fear of the sea. I've had a fear of the ocean ever since I was little. I have a hard time relaxing while floating because I think a sea monster is going to eat my feet or chew off an ear or I will spontaneously drown. Maybe my fear started when I was stung by a stingray once; maybe it was the time I almost drowned when I was past the wave break with my dad. Maybe it was when my dad tossed me into the deep end. But whatever the reason, I decide to let go of my fear of the ocean.

The waves are small enough that moving past the whitecaps and getting to the calm part of the water isn't too frightening. I move past them and lift my feet off the bottom and float. It's warm here. I fear jellyfish for a moment but then remind myself that I'm supposed to be releasing fear. I see a wave with a tiny whitecap out of the corner of my eye. I frantically make contact with the bottom and stand up. I can touch the bottom easily. It's shallow here. Something tells me to quit playing around; I'm fine. The sky is so exquisite that it can inject faith into the faithless. I lay my head back in the water and picture myself being baptized. I can hear the dolphins squeaking under the water. I grin and relax a bit more, knowing that where there are dolphins, there are rarely sharks. I stare up at the glorious sky and think about God, the universe, and if there is a higher purpose out there. I get the feeling that I'm protected. It is so stunning out here. I've never seen anything like this. It's as if St. Augustine is a sacred place. The clouds above me open up to reveal the moon. The sky seems to answer my question, or perhaps I'm reading into things too much. The waves are getting a tad higher, and out of the corner of my eye I spy whitecaps, and they're headed toward me. I start to freak. Here I am trying to release fear and I realize that I'm near the beach I used to go to with my dad when I was little. I'm out past the waves where my dad would take me. I stretch out my arms and remind myself that I am no longer a child. I can touch the bottom now. I relax.

All of a sudden, floating in the Atlantic Ocean I decide to trust in God even though I have always thought it was a bunch of hogwash. "If you're up there or around here or in here or whatever, I'll trust you. I trust you," I say out loud. I give my feet over to the monsters that will bite them off. I lay my palms open to feed whichever fish will nibble at them, and I wait to be dashed by a wave and drowned. Nothing happens. I just float. I'm floating out here and trusting, and nothing happens. There's no drama, and a two-headed monster does not swallow me up. I let go, and I trust. The whitecaps fade away and the waves coming toward me simply lift me up like I'm riding the back of a beast. I wonder if this moment is really happening or if my mind is making things up. A dolphin squeaks near me. "Is that you?" I ask. Who am I asking? God? I think of the other Angela Sheltons who spoke about God and how prayer has helped their lives. A wave lifts me up gently. The dolphins' squeaking sounds like giggles. Floating here feels like I'm being cradled, like I'm being reassured. "You can do anything. The only thing that holds you back is your fear. Let go of all your fear and feel only love. We have you, we are always here, and you are always protected. You are on a mission." I float and listen. I wonder if that really just happened. Did I hear that?

"Waves come all the time, every second. How am I to believe that this is some kind of message? How am I to believe that this is really God and not my brain making things up?" Right then I'm doused in the face with a whitecap that comes out of nowhere. I jump up coughing.

Day 44 of the search
Angela Shelton in South Carolina

"There's still a chance I can save her." My crew and I are passing through the town where the Angela Shelton that I lost lives. This is the one whose husbands beat her, and she thinks that her current husband won't hit her again. She's the one whose number was disconnected. I try her number again, naively thinking it might work since I'm here. "At the customer's request, this number has been disconnected." I search the phone book. I can't find her. I don't know why. I try the number again. It's been disconnected. I turn on the ignition and pull out of her town.

I pray that she finds a way out.

Day 45 of the search
Angela Shelton in South Carolina

My crew and I slowly cruise the streets of my father's town. Each one of us is jumpy, thinking my dad is going to walk around the corner at any moment. Charleston, South Carolina, is a quaint city and perfectly put together. We examine each family that passes and wonder what their secrets are. It feels like we're in another dimension in a way, as if denial is a disease and everyone has it, so no one knows he or she is sick.

My entire crew is cranky. I feel like I'm holding this ship together with dental floss. I'm anxiety-ridden and sad. Our next Angela Shelton is set to see us tomorrow, so we have the day off. I make promises of ice cream and stretch breaks, and I pay for extra snacks and a good restaurant. I wish I were alone. I find myself praying even though I don't really know how. God, help me keep this movie together. God, help me make it through this day, just this one day. Help me survive Charleston and then get me out of here.

1986

When I was about 14 my father sent me a box of presents. I was living in California with my mom. I hadn't heard from my father in years. He hadn't even sent child support. He hadn't called or tried to contact me. The mysterious package arrived on my doorstep. I thought that maybe my dad finally cared about me. It was exciting to receive a big box of presents from him. It was full of knickknacks like you get at a swap meet. I picked up a watch with a cartoon character on it, wrapped it around my wrist, and fastened it. I read the note he dropped into the box. He mentioned that he got married again. His new wife had two little kids. My heart stopped. "Hope you have a happy birthday, honey."

It took about five minutes before the watch cut my wrist. There was some kind of flaw on the back of it where the metal stuck out. Every time I moved, it sliced at my skin. My father's presents were trying to kill me. I took the watch along with the rest of the contents of the box and threw it in the trash. But I kept the note about his having two new children.

Day 46 of the search
Angela Shelton in South Carolina

"All these Angelas have represented stages of my own self-discovery," I recap for the Angela Shelton in my dad's town. She looks like a perfect Miss America. She's a young Caucasian woman with blonde hair, blue eyes, a gymnast's body, and a perfect white smile. "I see the circle I'm going in, the circle of Angelas. From the Angela in Washington who thought it was stupid to all the ones who told me to be independent and not rely on a man. The Angela in Detroit is all about having faith; the Angela in New York is about being strong, fighting back, and uniting. The one in Virginia has been to hell and back and yet is the most joyous Angela I've met. And now you—you believe a person has to report it and fight back through the system. It's so weird that you're tracking sexual predators and that my dad lives here. I mean . . ."

"Everything happens for a reason" Angela says.

"Practically every Angela has said that."

"Have they? Well, it's true."

"What do you think about my going to see my dad?"

"I think you really need to because in the end it's going to make you a better person."

"What do you think about all the Angela Sheltons who have been abused?" I flip through my binder of Angelas and scan all the ones I've interviewed. "Twenty-four out of 40 Angela Sheltons have been abused."

"I would ask what that says about women in general. I think the national statistics are way off because women tend to be silent about abuse."

"I know. What do we do about it?"

"A woman should have a plan in case bad things happen. Hopefully they never will, but you should still have a plan. Like with my husband, I told him when we got married that if he ever laid a hand on me that I would be out the door and never come back. You can't be a pushover. You have to have boundaries." She looks at me for a moment and then asks, "So people knew that your dad was abusing you and nobody ever filed charges?" She gets right to the subject. I picture her in a cop uniform filling out a report.

"Um, no. What happened is that my brother told his real dad and his real dad called social services. Then that same day social workers came and picked my sister and me up from school and took us directly to a foster care home. We never went home again. That was pretty traumatic."

"And he was never charged?" Angela asks again. That's always the question. Why wasn't my dad charged? I explain to her how the lawyers said it was best for us to be taken out of the house and not bother with a real trial because it would have been hard on us. "So he wasn't ever charged?" Angela asks again like she can't wrap her head around it.

"No. He was never caught. When he was married to my mom, he was a counselor in a boys' juvenile delinquent home and he was caught doing something, but I think he was only fired. There were other things he was caught for over the years, but there was never an official charge. He owned an arcade too."

I watch her shake her head from side to side slowly. "Predators are always in those types of jobs." I know full well that she knows that already.

"They're the kind of people you wouldn't think would do it. 'Oh, he's a good guy. He would never do that,'" she imitates the uninitiated.

"And he's always had a job where he traveled in a van."

"How frightening is that?"

"When I was a kid, he was the candy man. I remember his van filled with boxes of candy and toys that he used to fill the gumball machines."

"What a nightmare. And he's not the only one doing it either. That's the sad thing. We need to educate people more, and more of us need to take action."

1986

My dad married his third wife, a lady named Joy, when I was 14. Joy was younger than he and had two young boys. His new family received him well. He looked like a savior for marrying a single mother. After he sent me that box of presents for my birthday, he suggested that I come out for Christmas. I wasn't supposed to see him after being taken out of his house. That was the judge's order. My dad and my stepmother were not to have any contact with me. The order didn't say anything about his marrying other women who had kids though. My mother was not sure about my request to visit him. She didn't like the idea of my going all the way across the country to see him. I pleaded with her. I didn't care about seeing him or exchanging gifts with him. I wanted to talk to his wife. My mother didn't fight me on it; she never had rules before and tended to let me do what I wanted. She agreed to let me go if I promised to be careful.

I flew back to South Carolina to meet my dad and his new family. I knew what I was doing. I had a plan. My father was not inappropriate with me. He made no weird pass at me. He didn't ask me to get naked, and he didn't get naked in front of me. The household he was setting up with this new wife was different than it had been with my stepmother. I watched Joy's little boys. They were about 7 and 10 years old, maybe younger. Joy watched me watching them. I wondered if anything had already begun. I wondered how long it would take my dad before he started doing stuff. I waited for a moment alone with Joy. I gave her every opportunity to speak to me. One night we were sitting on the sofa watching TV. Her sons and my dad were asleep.

"Can I ask you something?" Joy leaned toward me. I looked at her. She was so pretty. I didn't understand why she would choose my dad. I also didn't expect the conversation to start like it did. "Why did your dad and his ex-wife divorce?" Joy scooted her feet up under herself on the couch. We both looked toward the bedroom she shared with my dad. The door was cracked. My dad's snoring could be heard all the way to the living room. It was safe to talk.

"Do you really want to know?" I asked her, and she nodded. "Um, well . . ." I faltered, but then I told her everything. "Do you know he used to take us to nudist camps?" She shook her head. She didn't know anything about his old life. "He started by having us get naked in the house. He led up to the other stuff. Me and Lisa had to jerk him off." Joy was horrified. "He taught us how to do it. He used to have us get naked all the time and take trips in his van to the nudist camps. We had to massage him and my stepmother too."

"Were they naked?"

"Yeah. He called them rubdowns." Joy looked toward the door where her new husband snored. I could tell she was thinking something. I had the feeling she already suspected something. I just stared at her. "We used to see them having sex. He showed us between her legs. He tried to get my stepbrother to have sex with her. But my stepbrother told his real dad and his real dad called social services, and we were taken out of the house and put into a foster home." Joy sat there quietly and listened. I'm not sure if she ever moved. "And then my stepmother stayed with him for years. I never understood it." Joy looked like I told her exactly what she needed to hear. We both sat quietly for a moment after I was done. Then we both got up and went to bed as if nothing was ever said.

The next day I flew back to California where I lived with my mom. My dad and his new family drove me to the airport and waved goodbye to me. I sat in the airplane and wondered if Joy was going to do anything about my dad or if she was going to pretend that our conversation never happened.

A week or so later my father called me. My mother came in and handed me the phone in a disgusted manner. "It's your father." I grabbed it.

"Hey, Dad."

"Hey, honey. How was your trip back?"

"Good. How is Joy? How are the boys?"

"That's why I'm calling. The weirdest thing happened, honey. I just don't know what to do. I mean I've hired a private detective and everything." He stammered and then trailed off. He was upset.

"What happened?"

"Joy took the kids. She left me. It was right after you went home. She even cleaned out our joint bank account. I think she has about $8,000," he sighed, defeated. I sat there listening while a grin spread across my face.

"Wow."

Thank you, Joy. For children everywhere, thank you.

Day 47 of the search
Father's Day in South Carolina

It's Father's Day morning. I get up and get dressed. I put on my *Searching for Angela Shelton* T-shirt and my oldest pair of Converse high-tops. I click on the "Dad" belt buckle that I bought for myself as a joke the day before I left on the trip. I figured it could represent me as the boss on the trip. I didn't realize it was a premonition. I clip Lori's piece-of-heart pin in my hair. We pick the South Carolina Angela Shelton up on our way to my dad's house. She lives about five miles from him. She holds the map while I drive.

"How do you feel, Ang?" Gallo asks.

"Um . . . I don't know. I'd be fine if you all wanted to skip this." Nobody laughs.

"What do you want to get out of this?" Gallo asks, camera pointed at me.

"To be honest, I would really like to know what happened to him. I want to know where the links in the chain started."

Angela Shelton tells me to turn right. I feel sick. My skin is breaking out by the minute and my heart is racing. We turn down my dad's street, and I see a van, but it isn't his. Then I see another van and another one, but none of them are my dad's. Then I see his van parked in his driveway. It is the same one he had a few years ago that was filled with Beanie Babies. I wonder how many other child molesters live on this street. I park the RV across the street from his house. It is Sunday morning. People are leaving for church. I figure he'll be doing the same soon. Giovanni wires me, and I step out of the RV, close the door, and stand there. I know my crew is waiting at the window to watch me walk toward my dad's door. I am frozen. I'm on the other side of the RV across the street from my father's house. He can't see me even if he is looking out the window. I am suddenly very afraid. I'm scared that my legs won't carry me across the grass that covers his front yard.

"God, give me strength. God, give me strength," I pray as I stand there by the door. I don't even know why I'm praying. I've never prayed before. I feel like this is all a dream and there's nothing to be afraid of because this really isn't happening. Am I going crazy? "God, give me strength. God, give me strength," I repeat as I step out into the street and make my way across my dad's front yard, up his front steps, and to his front door.

I ring the bell. My dad opens the door so quickly that I stammer for a second and then quickly announce, "Happy Father's Day!"

"What in the world?" He is as shocked as I am. "How are you?" He has already started to tear up.

"Good."

"Give me a hug," he says. I go to hug him. He is my dad. It is like I am on autopilot. As he pulls me to him, he moves to kiss me straight on the lips with his mouth parted. I turn my face just in time and present him with my cheek instead. I'm not sure what just happened. Did my dad just try to kiss me on the mouth?

"What are you doing, sweetheart?"

"I'm traveling around the country making a movie about myself." I laugh uncomfortably and show him my T-shirt. He makes a proud papa face and then notices my belt buckle and grimaces.

"Well, come on in. You got your husband with you?"

"No, I'm divorced," I say and laugh again. I wonder how he knows I was married. Then I remember the letter I wrote him ages ago. I realize that he must have read it.

"Is that yours?" He points toward the RV.

"My whole film crew is in there. We're making a movie," I remind him and wave toward the RV.

"Oh my. Well, come in." I step into my father's house. It looks like any other house in America. The curtains match the upholstery. There are knickknacks on polished shelves. The candles have never been lit. They match the curtains. I sit down on the sofa that faces the TV. "My wife is getting ready for church. Let me go put on a shirt." He moves off down the hallway to put on something over his undershirt. It reminds me of all the times he yelled at us to get naked. His wife comes out while he's gone. She is very plain. I wonder how my dad ever ended up with a beautiful woman like my mother. I figure her low self-esteem was probably to blame.

"Oh, honey, your father talks about you every day, every day," his wife says as she grabs my hands and holds onto them. "It is so good to meet you." She smiles her fake Southern smile that women here do so well.

"Thank you." I smile right back. I am also Southern.

"I just want to let you know that no matter what happens, your daddy loves you." I wonder what she means by that. Did she read the letter too? Does she know about his past? "I am just so glad that you're here." I wonder if she's serious. She looks like she's lying, and she's not very good at it. She's not as good as my dad. I think about telling her that I'm here to get my dad to fess up to being a child molester, but he walks back into the room. "Well, I'm going to go get ready," his fourth wife says as if it's her cue. She moves off down the hallway and leaves me alone with my dad. He comes over and sits down on the sofa next to me.

"It is so good to see you, Angie," he says and coughs up tears. I want to roll my eyes and slap him, but I don't. "I've missed you so much. I've thought about you every day, every day," he sighs, as if he rehearsed it. "I'm so proud of you, honey." He touches my knee. I move my leg and he takes his hand away. "And your movie, I thought it was just so great."

"Thanks. I'm making another one." I figure he must be talking about *Tumbleweeds*.

"I see that." He looks at my T-shirt and then glances down at my "Dad" belt buckle. He looks away quickly.

"I'm traveling around the country meeting women named Angela Shelton and hearing their stories, and I realized that I needed to tell mine." My dad looks worried all of a sudden. He glances back down at my belt buckle again.

"What's the Dad belt for?"

"All roads lead to you, Dad."

He sits back on the sofa as if preparing himself for an interrogation. "OK, all right, OK." His shoulders twitch. "But, honey, some of that stuff you wrote in that letter, some of it wasn't true."

"Why didn't you respond to my letter?"

"Honey, I didn't know how. You just had these god-awful, gothic thoughts of me," he stammers. "I mean, I made some stupid mistakes. The nudist camp did us in." He shakes his head and looks at his hands. I wonder what he means by that, but I'm too busy staring at him moving his arms about, sweating, and wiping his tears away to ask. I wonder what my crew is thinking right now, huddled around Giovanni's earphones. "When you moved away, I just fell apart." He's trying to get me to feel sorry for him, I can tell. "I loved you so much," he says and wipes a tear.

"I love you too, Dad."

He stops and turns to me, his eyes full of tears. "Do you? Do you really? That means so much to me." I want to tell him that he should get an agent. He's such a good actor. I wonder if he ever took acting classes; maybe he missed his calling. "I mean, what happened to us?" He cries and looks up at the ceiling like he's in a Shakespeare play.

I want to tell him that if he loved me, he would have sent child support to my mother. He would have tracked me down. He would have sent my mom and me coal when we lived in the house with the coal stove and had no money to fill it. He would have called or shown up or checked in. I want to get angry and yell at him. I want to run down the hallway and shake his wife by her shoulders and tell her she's married to a sex offender. But he seduces me with his tears and I stay quiet. My father is pathetic.

"I have to forgive you," I say more to myself than to him.

"Do you think somewhere down the road you can do that?" He coughs and wipes his face.

"I sort of need to hear it from you."

"Well, tell me what you need to know."

I don't know where to start. I stumble around the words in my head. "You molested—"

"I did not," he jumps in. "I did not. I swear. I never laid a hand on you. I never, never, never, never, never laid a hand on you," he says while shaking his head from side to side.

"I know you didn't," I assure him. He stops acting and looks at me. "I only had to do stuff when Lisa was in the room. But you used to take her into the room by herself," I remind him. I'm annoyed that it's easier to bring up what he did to Lisa than what he did to me. And he didn't touch me; I had to touch him. His manipulation is getting to me, and it's infuriating.

"And Steven," he tosses out. "I don't know what happened with Steven. I didn't have anything to do with him becoming gay," he professes. I didn't even mention Steve. I wonder if I'm dealing with a certifiable lunatic. "We made the stupid mistake of running around naked," my dad says. I hear the word "we" and wonder who else he is trying to pin his abuse on. I stare at him sweating on his sofa that matches his curtains. "I mean God strike me dead this very instant, this very instant—10 minutes until 10 a.m.—if I did it." He splays his arms open, closes his eyes, and turns his face up toward the ceiling. I lean back from him just in case a lightning bolt breaks through the roof and splits the sofa in two. My dad turns to me. He's crying when he says, "I am not lying to you." I have such a desire to lift one of these matching lamps on the polished end table and whack him over the head with it, but I just stare at him instead. I wonder how many perpetrators have jobs as salesmen.

"We should go outside. My crew is waiting."

"OK," he says like he's getting a closeup. "Now, honey, are you going to make me out to be the villain?"

"You're telling me that you're not the villain, so how can I make you out to be one?" He doesn't say anything. "I'm going across the street, and I'll be back with my cameraman."

"I'll go wash my face." He starts to walk away and then turns and adds, "Honey, it's so good to see you."

I just stare at him. I don't even smile. I just look at him and then turn toward his front door. I need to get out of there. I am starting to feel the walls slide in toward me. I walk down his front steps, across the grass and the street, and around to the door of the motor home, cursing the whole way. "I can't believe how pissed off I am. I am so pissed off. I am so pissed off!" I swing the door open. Angela Shelton and my crew are sitting there staring at me wide-eyed as I barrel inside.

"It's OK, calm down, calm down. You're doing great," Gallo tells me.

"You need to hit him with the facts," Chantal reminds me.

"He's so lying. He's just sitting there lying to you," Angela says. "I love the 'god-awful, gothic things.'" They have one of Giovanni's extra headsets that they've been passing around so they could hear what went on inside the house.

"So he's coming out on the porch to talk."

"Get him to sign a release," Gallo reminds me.

"He will. Did you hear him ask me if I was going to make him into a villain? Asshole." After I compose myself and take a deep breath, I grab a release. Gallo and I head back to my dad's house. The door is already cracked open, so I just push it open wider.

"Hey, this is Gallo, my cameraman," I tell my dad as he scurries toward the door, buttoning his shirt.

"Hey, how you doing?" He goes to shake Gallo's hand. I can tell Gallo wants to punch him in the face. "Good to see you." My dad smiles with that Southern charm oozing off of him.

Gallo just nods sternly. "Happy Father's Day."

"What a Father's Day." My dad shakes his head.

"You know what? Do you have one that's not striped?" I ask, pointing to his shirt.

"Yep, that would do better, right?"

"Because it will—"

"It'll blur," he says, finishing my sentence for me.

"Yeah." I wonder if my dad has been on TV before. "Welcome to hell," I say to Gallo as my dad heads down the hallway to grab another shirt. We shut the door and come out on the porch.

"You're doing good," Gallo says. I appreciate his tenderness. Even though they are my crew, they have grown into family and I'm glad I'm not here alone.

My dad comes outside wearing a new shirt. I hand him the release to sign. He signs it. "Now, you're not making me out to be the bad guy, are you?" I laugh as he hands me the signed release, and I put it in my bag.

I don't know what to say to him. He is digging his own hole. Gallo takes a Polaroid and heads back to the RV with the camera. My dad and I sit on his front steps. I don't want a camera in our faces. I want to feel like we're alone. I charge right in, thinking that if I don't, I will never get it out of my mouth. "I saw Steven and Lisa."

"You did?" My dad holds onto the Polaroid that Gallo just took of us. "How are they?"

"They're good. I asked Steve to tell me what you did to him."

My dad rocks his big head from side to side. "Are we back on that subject? I don't know what made Steve become gay; I never touched him."

"What about offering his mother to him?"

"Now that was a joke. I remember there was a time when Steven showed himself off to one of the girls visiting." My father is a genius at diverting attention from himself.

"I wonder where he got that from?" I throw in, but my dad ignores it and goes on. He's stammering.

"I told him if he was going to expose himself, then he should expose himself to his mother. That's what I said. I didn't offer him to his—" he cuts himself off. I watch his face. His mind is racing. I have a flashback of him going ballistic, punching walls, throwing things, and yelling. I remember the time he punched a hole in Steve's bedroom door. He put his fist right through it. I hate that he used his anger, that we were all so afraid of him because of it. I want to hit him, but I just sit there. I decide to hit him with words instead.

"What about when Lisa and I had to jerk you off? Do you remember that?"

My dad shakes his head no. "I remember one time, and it wasn't jerked off. I was never jerked off. There was a picture or something that we took. No, it wasn't a picture. It wasn't a picture," he repeats as if trying to convince himself. I think about Steve telling me about the Polaroids my dad used to take of us. I look at the one he's holding in his hand and wonder where that album is. I figure he got rid of it a long time ago. I'm starting to see that I'm going to get nowhere with my dad. He is a professional manipulator. "There was a rubdown involved, and that was the last time," my dad continues. He shakes his head, like he isn't buying his own lies. "But there was no jerking off, and when you put in that letter that you were there . . ." He waves his arm as if this is all nonsense.

"I was there. I remember that. That was when I was in the room with Lisa. The rest of the time she was alone in the room." I turn toward him. He shakes his head.

"You both were fully clothed," he says, and I wonder if he realizes how ridiculous he sounds.

I have a flashback of us naked. I consider stopping, rewinding, and bringing that up. But he's going to continue to lie no matter what. I remember my mother telling me that he would deny everything as she sat on the swing next to my grandmother.

"Yep," my father nods like he can read my mind. I look over at him. "There was no ejaculation though," he proclaims. "I don't even remember you being there, but there was no ejaculation, period." I just stare at him. I am utterly amazed. I'm amazed that this fat liar is the person I have desperately wanted as my father all these years. I'm amazed that because he was not a good father that I have sought out men who did not really want me. I'm amazed at how much control our parents have over us. I'm amazed that I am not jumping up and down, screaming at him right now. I'm amazed that he got away with it. "I mean that's vile," he says and turns to me. "I made the stupid mistakes about the nudist colonies and running around with our clothes off." He looks down at his hands.

"Yeah, but there's nothing wrong with that," I say but want to correct myself. I think nudist colonies are gross and a breeding ground for perpetrators. As I sit here and remember all the camps he brought us to as kids and all the other families, I wonder if those nudist camps weren't meeting places for him and his perp friends. I wonder if that's where he went to learn new techniques. He is stammering. I wonder if I'm going to get a taste of his temper. He seems like he's getting riled up. I remember that Giovanni is in the RV with his tomahawk. I grin, picturing Gio running across my dad's lawn with his tomahawk raised above his head, screaming in his Italian accent. "Nudist colonies are sick, a bunch of sickos." I don't know what else to say. My dad nods like he's agreeing with me. He must be crazy. Then he shakes his head quickly as if he just realized he doesn't want to agree with me.

"The thing is that it's almost like the story of Halley's comet," my dad begins to explain. I stare at him. Halley's comet? My father is reaching for the stars, literally. "You know, where somebody sees something in the sky and doesn't know what it is, and then all of a sudden the object gets to where it's a piece of the moon or a piece of another planet falling to Earth. The story just keeps growing and growing." He waves his hands like he has the whole universe figured out.

I'm flooded with a memory of swimming to him with the sharks around. I wonder if I can just get up and walk away from this moment. I wonder if I can just decide to not have a dad. I remember floating in the ocean a few days ago. I think about God. I wonder if I really am protected. I wonder what I'm doing sitting here. What do I even want from this man? "I don't know, I don't know," my dad sighs, shaking his head from side to side. "It's just that over the years, after all these years, this is like a kitten that has all of a sudden become a tiger." I roll my eyes and let my hands fall. I give up. My father really has missed his calling as an actor.

"Do you know what Steve used to do to us?" I'm trying a different angle. At this point I have given up on getting my dad back. I'm thinking about my movie. I want him to continue talking. He is digging his own hole to lie down in.

"The only thing I ever knew is that he said he had tried to do something with you one time, but no, I don't know anything else," he admits. I wonder when he would have heard Steve say such a thing. Then I remember that all the kids had to get on the stand, but we weren't allowed to be in the courtroom at the same time. I didn't get to hear what Lisa and Steve said in court. I was the last to take the stand.

"It was constant. We played games. We gave him head. He gave us head."

"Are you serious?" My father drops his hands and shakes his head from side to side again and again.

"He put the broom handle up his ass," I continue. "He put the handle of the mirror up his ass and would walk around."

"Oh, Angie . . ." my dad sighs. We sit in silence for a moment.

"And at 12 years old, I don't think you just do that." My dad stops shaking his head suddenly. "I mean, you don't just wake up one day and say, 'I want to put a broom handle up my ass.'"

"Where are you saying he got that from?"

"I'm wondering." I turn and stare right at him. If I can't get the words out of my mouth, I'll stare it out of him.

"I didn't do anything. I swear to God, Li—I mean Angie. Damn," he stammers, catching his mistake. He rubs the sweat off his brow. I look at the camera. Did he almost just call me Lisa? I wonder what Lisa would say about that. I wonder if he's thinking about her deep down. I wonder if he regrets what he did to her. I wonder if my crew is upset with me for just sitting here and not screaming at him. He's sweating and his eyes are darting all over the place. He plays with the Polaroid in his hand.

"It would make perfect sense why Steve would do that stuff and why we kids would play games like that. We were being abused, and everyone was always naked in the house, and stuff was always going on."

"I never abused you as a child," my dad says harshly and turns to face me. "Now you're saying Steven did all this stuff?" I want to squeeze his fat head until it bursts. "I'm not trying to be a psychiatrist here or a psychologist. But if all this stuff really did happen, and I don't have any reason not to believe you . . ." My eyebrows wrinkle on that comment. Can he hear himself? Does he know how crazy he sounds? "Then over time," he continues. "I've become the so-called villain, and to you it was me, subconsciously, instead of Steven."

"No," I state simply. I want to scream and beat him about his head and shoulders. Child molesters lie. They manipulate, and they lie. They try to make you think that you are the crazy one.

I wonder what my dad will say when I send him a copy of this movie and he gets a good look at himself.

"I did not do it," he reminds me.

"I have a distinct memory. On the waterbed, the green shag carpet, the A-frame, in the hallway, standing there, and your wife opened the door. She sent Lisa in there, and you're on the bed, naked. And she shut the door and took me away so I didn't hear anything." I'm annoyed at how all of a sudden I can't speak English properly. I feel like I'm in quicksand and can't remember the technique to get out.

"I don't know why or where that came from." My dad turns to me, looks me in the eye, and says flatly, "But, Angie, that did not happen." My blood is boiling. I want to poke his eyes out with my fingers. Did he just flat-out lie straight to my face? "I did not do it. No . . . No . . . I don't know, I don't know," he says over and over, shaking his head back and forth, sweating. He sounds like a broken record, and he makes me sick. "I've always heard that there's such a strong relation between brother and sister . . ." He trails off like he's searching for the next tall tale. He continues a long monologue about how he didn't do anything, and Steve must have done everything, and I'm just remembering everything incorrectly. "You can put it on my tombstone. 'I did not do it.' And I would not be the least bit afraid," he assures me. "Because I didn't do it, and I am not going to sit here and admit to something just to make you feel better. Not when I swear to God that I didn't do it." When he says "swear to God" he makes quotation marks in the air with his fingers like he's mocking the divine. I lean away from him, half expecting a lightning bolt to charge forth from the sky. "I want what is best for you and I hope someday that you can purge all of this."

"I'm purging," I assure him.

"Are you?" He looks me over and puts on the actor's face of a concerned father. "Can I ask what you're purging?"

"That I cannot rely on anyone but myself and that I must parent myself," I state flatly. He stares at me. I don't think that was what he wanted to hear.

"All right," he sighs. I assume at this point that my crew is furious with me for not whacking him over the head with my bag or kicking him in the crotch and taking off toward the RV. I give up. I do not have a father. This fat man sitting next to me is a big, lying bastard. I'm disappointed because if he did come clean I would be open to having a relationship with him. It could be like it was with Steve. We could have a relationship on some level, but instead he is trying to pin blame on my stepbrother. My father is a liar. I turn and glare at him.

"You lie," I say accusatorially.

"What? About what?"

"We're a lot alike, you and I, on one level. We're both actors. You're a great manipulator."

"Manipulate? I am not a manipulator, as such." The "as such" rings in my head.

"Yes, you are. You've always been a salesman."

"Well, yeah." He quickly changes the subject. "Do you all remember when I was driving that van that had all them toys in the back?" I nod and wonder why he addressed me as "you all." I wonder if he thinks he's addressing all the kids he abused by talking to me. Is my father a schizo? "And there was one little plastic boy. He was peeing, and the company recalled it because of his little thingy sticking out." He laughs, making a little penis with his finger to help his story out. Here I am trying to confront my father for molesting us, and he's talking about little penises on plastic boy toys. "And we had to get in that van and look through all those boxes and find all those little peeing boys," he continues. "We never did find any, did we?" I stare at him. My father is a lunatic.

"I love you, you know," he says and turns to me and puts his hand on my knee. "I want us to go forward. I want to know about your modeling, and I'd love for you to send me some pictures of you, some modeling pictures." I cannot believe he just said that. Is he joking? Did my child molester father just ask me for modeling pictures? I don't understand why I am not wailing on him. I stare at the camera. Are the rest of you hearing this? Do you see this crazy manipulation happening? "I was flipping through the channels one night and saw you on TV. You were on *Becker,* and I'd love to know about things like that. I really would." I'm not listening to him anymore. He makes me ill. It is so sick and twisted to think about him watching me on TV. I can just see him hanging out with all his nudist freak friends, telling them about what he used to do to us. I wonder how many modeling pictures he has of me. I want to barf. I wonder if he still has that other album of us as kids hidden somewhere under his perfectly polished floorboards. I feel gross that I'm even sitting here next to him. I'm frozen. I wonder if I'm reverting back to being a little girl. Is this disassociation? Am I scared of this man? I know he has a violent temper. I've seen it. I want to yell at him, but it's not worth it. His denial will only make me angrier, and then I'll be pegged the lunatic. If I did freak out on him, I could be carted off by the authorities as he repeats, "I didn't do it. I didn't do it."

"I'm not stupid enough," my father says like he knows my thoughts. "I want you, and I want you in my life, but I'm not going to sit here and admit to something to make you feel better. That's a promise in blood. Our blood." I want to slit my wrists right there on his doorstep and drain his blood out of me. "I did not do it," he repeats. I look over at him and think about all the times I self-mutilated, scratched myself, hit myself, beat myself up when I really should have wailed on my father.

"You're driving me crazy," I say quietly.

"Well, it's driving me crazy," he says back just as quietly. He probably doesn't even realize how true that is.

"All I wanted was some closure with you. And for you to . . ."

"That's what I'm trying to do, but it's just not true. I did not do it, and that's all I can say. Jesus Christ," he sighs. I remember that his latest wife is inside getting ready for church. She's probably putting on her lipstick right now that matches her earrings and her nails. I picture the two of them putting on a grand show for all their fellow churchgoers. I wonder what Jesus would say about all of this.

"All right, well, I'll let you go to church."

"Well, listen. It's just a dad thing, but be careful," he warns. A dad thing? When was he ever my dad? "And please enjoy life," he adds. I want to kick him.

"I do. Very much."

"You have a beautiful life ahead of you, and I'm very proud of you. But, honey, I'll say it one more time. I'm not going to say it again because I've said it enough." He pauses. I already know what he's going to say. "I did not do it," he spits out as I expected. I stand up and he follows my lead. "Where are you going from here?"

"Georgia."

"Honey, thank you for being here. And someday wipe the slate clean." He hugs me goodbye. I do not hug him back. I just stand there and clutch my bag.

"Happy Father's Day," I say again just before I head back toward the RV and my sperm donor goes back inside to his perfectly upholstered living room. I feel like my feet are not touching the ground as I head back toward the RV. Someone opens the door before I have a chance to. I step in and sit down. My crew just stares at me. I say nothing. I'm in shock. I'm angry, and I feel like if I even so much as grimace, I will start ripping the sides of the RV off. So I sit down and I don't move. Chantal hands me a bottle of water. Angela Shelton stares at me.

"I can't believe he just lied like that," she says. "He's not in denial. He's just a liar."

"Why didn't you freak out on him, Ang?" Gallo first asks the question I was expecting. "I can't believe you didn't wail on him."

"You handled it a lot differently than I would have," Angela says. "I think I would have hit him."

"Now the real work begins, Angelina," Giovanni says. I look at him. "You need to move on. Now you need to forgive." I want to throw something. I don't have to forgive anything.

"What were you thinking while you sat there?" Gallo asks. "You just sat there."

"That I don't have a father. That I wish I had a dad. I really wanted him to be my dad. I wanted the visit to be like it was with Steve. But I realized I need to parent myself."

Chantal nods. Sylvia cries. "I hate him. I just hate him," she peeps out. "I can't believe he just sat there and lied to you. I can't believe it."

"But it's what I do now that is important, right?" They all nod. Chantal and Gallo both offer to drive, but I want to be behind the wheel. I pull away from my father's house. I pass the other vans on his street one by one and wonder how many other families share the same secret. I'm sick of talking about the past. I'm sick of how much it has affected my life and how much time it has stolen from me. I want to drive toward the future.

PART II

THE JOURNEY HOME

July 4, 2001 – Independence Day
Two months after the search

I recognize the area code when the phone rings. I let it ring three times before answering it. I'm not really sure if I want to spend my day talking to an alcoholic.

"Hey there, Angela Shelton Anonymous." I call the alcoholic Angela Shelton by the nickname I've given her to help keep her hidden. I'm not in the mood for her right now, but she's become like an old friend at this point, and I haven't heard from her in a month.

"I figured it was appropriate that I call you right now." She sounds different. She's not slurring. I wonder what number beer she's on. Maybe she just opened the case.

"It's good to hear from you. How are you doing? It's been awhile."

"It has been 28 days. I just got out of rehab. I'm sober now." I almost fall off the steps I'm sitting on. "And you told me to not call you until I was sober."

"Oh my God, Angela, that's awesome. Really? Good for you. Wow, really?"

"Yeah. I went in right after the last time we talked." I am too shocked to respond. I'm amazed at how different she sounds. "I wore my *Searching for Angela Shelton* T-shirt the entire time in rehab too. Everyone got a kick out of that."

"Wow, that's perfect, searching for Angela Shelton for real. That's so amazing that you went to rehab. What made you go into rehab?"

"After the last time we talked I went on a three-day drunk. I don't remember much of that weekend. I wrecked my car and blacked out. A friend drove me to the center but I refused to go in. I was so drunk by the time I got in there that I was at the very end. But when I started to sober up, things started to make sense. I had hit rock bottom. I feel a lot different now. I'm not sick all the time for one thing."

"Or drunk."

"Or drunk, yeah," she laughs. "And I'm able to laugh again and talk to people without being drunk, which is really wonderful."

"Wow. I'm so happy to get this call. It's so nice to hear your voice sober. You sound so different."

"Yeah," Angela sighs like she's remembering all of her drunken nights. "I'm really sorry. I'm sorry that you were on my drunk dial list."

"That's okay. Everything happens for a reason."

"You were meant to make that movie. I believe you came into my life for a reason. I think that was meant to happen. It really started me thinking. I had gotten into such a rut, and you shook things up a bit. You changed my life. You woke me up."

"Waking up is a good way to put it. But that wasn't me who did that—that was you."

"God brought you. I believe that now. It took me awhile, but I saw that I wasn't alone. That was the most helpful part, knowing that I wasn't alone. I always thought I was the only one. So I wanted you to be the first person I called when I got out of rehab. I just wanted to say thank you to Angela Shelton."

"Thank you, Angela Shelton! Talking to you has really been me talking to myself in a lot of ways too. You have had a bigger effect on me than you even know. Hopefully this movie has a good effect on other people like it did on us."

"I'm excited to see it. When can I see it? When will you be finished?"

"I have no idea. I haven't even started putting all the pieces together. I just got back home."

Day 48 of the search
Somewhere in South Carolina

"I just saw my dad," I tell my therapist from a pay phone on the street. It is hot as hell. The rain has stopped. We just pulled over at a Dairy Queen on some tiny road in the middle of nowhere. My crew is inside ordering ice cream sundaes.

"Ah . . ." my therapist sighs. "And how was that?"

"He denied everything. It made me crazy. He just sat there and denied everything, but then he said that there was no ejaculation."

"Oh my."

"And I can see it as plain as day. It was the white stuff that came out of his thingy." Just saying that makes me feel like I'm 6 years old again. I want to put my fist through the side of the phone booth.

"By him denying it and not looking at what he did, does that make your reality seem altered?" I nod as if she can see me through the telephone. "By him not taking responsibility for his actions, is that what makes you feel crazy?"

"Yes, that's exactly how I feel, like I'm crazy. Do they all do this? I mean really. How many other abusers are out there lying to the faces of their victims?" I think of the alcoholic Angela and her cases of beer and how her father lied to her daily by telling her she was lower than a dog.

"Are you taking care of yourself? I know you're on the road, but are you giving yourself any kind of break? You need to give yourself some time to sit with this."

"No, I haven't really. I have to drive." I don't buy my excuse any more than she does.

"Maybe tonight you can get a room of your own. Get away from everyone for a while. You need to digest what happened. You're doing a lot all at the same time. You really need to take some time to sit with this. The world is not going to collapse if you take some time to process."

I glance toward the Dairy Queen at my crew inside eating ice cream. For a split second I think about running back to the RV, leaving all of them there, and hightailing it back home by myself. I want to scream all the way back to California. I clutch the phone receiver instead and stare down the road, thinking about how much further I have to go physically and mentally. I am agitated. I feel like flipping out. I want to scream and yell and jump up and down and kick something. But I don't. I stand holding the phone and watching my crew eat ice cream. I have a flashback of being forced to sit with my sister in the back of my foster mother's car as she took her real son into the ice cream parlor. She sat by the window with her son, eating ice cream cones while Lisa and I watched from inside her hot car. Bitch.

"How are you feeling?" my therapist asks.

"Fine," I lie. I sound like the alcoholic Angela. "I'm almost done searching for Angela Shelton." I laugh it off. We make an appointment for me to go see her when I get back to Los Angeles and I hang up the phone. My shoulders ache. I stand outside the RV and wait for my crew. I don't feel like having an ice cream cone at the moment.

Nine months after the search
Postproduction, Los Angeles

I did not believe that I could put my movie together myself, so I handed it over to a man. He's a flamboyant gay man, so I figure he has just the right combination of masculine and feminine qualities. I met him through Giovanni. I think he's perfect to put my movie together for me. I handed all 127 tapes that we shot on the road over to him and washed my hands of the trip, the movie, and my dad. My living room is filled with a huge editing system that I rented on a promise of funds to come. The Angela Shelton binder lies open on the table. All the pages are dog-eared, wrinkled, and full of Polaroids. You can't really be in my house without being faced with this movie, so I leave as much as I can. I go on acting auditions to try to make more money to keep my editor paid. I write a TV show. I hike with my dog.

As I pass the editing system on my way out again, my editor stops me. "Honey bunny," he says as he twirls the chair around to face me. "I know that you said you want this movie to focus on all the other Angela Sheltons, but this movie is about you." I look at him like he has lost his mind. I had instructed him to do a montage of all the Angelas and their stories. I want to show what they do for a living, whether they're married or single, if they have kids, if they went to school, and then cut to what they've been through in their lives. I want to bring up that most of them have been victims, but I want the majority of the movie filled with them saying really inspirational things to women. That seems simple enough. I want to inspire women. I don't see why I have to include my story to do that.

"There's no way to cut around you, honey bunny. It has to be about you. We want to know more about you. The other Angelas are great, but we care about you, how you are, what happens to you."

I need to lie down. I feel like I did when I found out that the Angela Shelton in my dad's town was tracking sexual predators. This strange numbness moves across my chest. I just nod to my editor. I know he's right, and I hate it. I want to be lazy and ignore my story and continue to hide. I feel like I have so much more work to do on myself that I want to accelerate my healing. I know that involves finishing this movie. I can hear the Angelas in my head saying that everything happens for a reason, and I want to poke my eyes out to make them shut up. My editor gets back to work, and I head into my bedroom. I climb onto my bed and lie there staring at the ceiling. I'm a wreck. I want to escape. I want this to go faster. I want to be done already. The phone rings and it is Angela Shelton Anonymous.

"Jesus Christ, can't you leave me alone?" I say to the ceiling. I pick up the phone anyway. Angela provides a great distraction from my own pain.

"Hey," she says and continues with, "I'm drunk," before I can respond.

"Really? I thought you got sober. I thought you went to rehab." I sit up in bed. Angela kind of huffs like that was a crackpot idea.

"Yeah, well," she mumbles.

I'm not in the mood for this. I'm feeling lower than a dog myself at the moment. Just hearing her voice makes me want a cigarette. I get up with my cordless phone and grab the pack that I have hidden from myself. I head outside. "One day we'll have to be nice to ourselves, Angela," I suggest as I light up.

"I know I'm abusing myself."

"At least you admit it."

"But there's no way out." I exhale and think about my movie. "My dad's getting ready to die," Anonymous Angela lets slip out, and I realize why she's drinking again.

"Really? Do you think that sort of lets him off the hook?" She isn't listening. She has run off down memory lane.

"I'm doing his laundry," she says softly.

"Yeah, that's for sure, his dirty laundry. It's amazing how we have to pick up the pieces when someone else shatters the glass." That was good, I think. I should write that down. I should write another TV show. My mind starts to drift to all the things I can work on besides my movie.

"No, I'm really doing his laundry," Angela says after a pause.

"You still see him?"

"Of course. That's just perfect, huh?"

"Have you ever mentioned anything to him? Have you ever confronted him?" I can't understand how she could be near that man. I want to punch him, and I've never even met him.

"Oh no. I could never," she says, and I have a flashback to me sitting right next to my dad. There are even pictures of him hugging me. Gross.

"What would you say to him if you could?"

"What would I say to my father?" It sounds like she never thought of that before. "Oh, gosh. That I wish . . ." she trails off as if stepping onto the train that passes her house periodically. "Don't hurt me, okay? Don't hurt me," she peeps out in a little girl voice.

"Angela, I'm not going to hurt you. I'm too busy hurting myself." I light a cigarette off the one I have in my hand. I listen to her pause and sip her beer.

"What did you really think of me when you met me?" She changes the subject.

"I thought you were adorable."

"You are so full of it."

"It's true. You are adorable. You have the cutest way about you. It's amazing how we beat ourselves up because of what someone else did to us."

"It's the only way I know."

"I do the same thing. There are so many ways of hiding it too." I look into the window of my house and see my editor at work in my living room. "It's like we're hiding from ourselves. I'm outside smoking when I have asthma and know it's killing me. And my editor is in there cutting this movie, and I know in my gut that I'm going to have to cut it myself, but I'm too scared to admit it."

"You should."

"I can't. I don't know how to work the machine." Angela is quiet. I listen to her take a few swigs and drags.

"I guess that's what my alcoholism is. It's the total blanket I'm hiding under." She pops open a new can.

"Wow, you phrase that so well. You should write that one down."

"I wish I was a writer like you."

"Just write then. You can do it. Why do you hide under the blanket of alcoholism?"

"Because when I'm drunk I can speak."

"You don't have to use alcohol," I say but already know that is easier said than done. I'm a hypocrite. Angela has her beer, I chain-smoke, I beat myself up, and I tend to go after men who don't like me. They are all secrets we hide so well.

"I have to be drunk. I'm not pretty or intelligent or artistic. That's why I'm attracted to people like you, Angela Shelton." She sighs quietly like she's letting our name sink in for the first time. "I'm so ugly. And stupid. I'm just lower than a dog." That's exactly how I feel right now, but I don't tell her that.

"Good grief, Angela. I wish you'd shut up about that. I'm so sick of hearing about the lower-than-a-dog syndrome. You are absolutely adorable and you can do anything you want. You're just stopping yourself." I should say all of this into a mirror 100 times.

"But you're so pretty, Angela."

"Oh, please. You always say that, but you know what? When I walk by the mirror my first thought is eww," I confess.

"Really? Me too."

"That is just sad. I wish you could see yourself. We need to get those negative voices out of our heads." I take another drag of my cigarette.

"I wish I could get better," Angela says quietly.

"I know, me too." We sit there and smoke for a while in silence. I wonder what number beer she's on. I just want to go to sleep while the man in my living room cuts my movie. I realize something while sitting here in my backyard, holding the phone, and talking to myself. "You know what? Beating ourselves up and not loving ourselves only perpetuates what our abusers did to us. It's like we're letting them win over and over again. It's like we're spinning on some wheel of pain."

"I know. I just don't know how to stop it."

"Yeah, me neither." I smash out my cigarette and light another one.

Day 49 of the search
Angela Shelton in Georgia

"You have a long life ahead of you to be angry," the Angela Shelton in Georgia tells me. She helps people die. She isn't like Jack Kevorkian or anything; she is the clinical coordinator of a convalescent home. She counsels families and the elderly boarders about death and dying. I can't believe the synchronicity of this Angela dealing with death when I am going through a death of sorts.

"Don't you think it's interesting the order in which these Angelas have come? Seriously. The first Angela Shelton rented out space to a foster care company, and I was in a foster home as a child. That's weird. Then there's the Angela who tracks sexual predators and lives in the same town as my dad. And now the Angela right after I see my father helps people cope with death. It's like a metaphor for me to decide to live or something. A death of the old self and a rebirth of a new one."

"There is certainly some symbolism there," Angela says. "Do you believe in angels?" She looks at me so seriously that I know she's not joking.

"Yeah. I do. I believe in angels. I believe we're all angels."

"I believe in stuff like that," Angela admits. "And I think you have a mission and I think that God has a plan for us, and as soon as we've fulfilled that mission then we move on."

"I believe that. I wonder what my mission is."

"I believe you're fulfilling it right now with this movie you're making. It's never going to be over. It's more of a movement than a movie with what you're bringing up. You're giving women a platform, and you're highlighting a huge issue, and those conversations will continue with or without you. This isn't about the Angelas. You are talking about everyone." I stare at her. Why are the Angelas so perceptive?

As Angela walks through the halls, the elderly and her staff look at her with respect and a bit of awe. Perhaps they can see a halo around her head. I follow Angela into her office. "I see a lot of suffering," Angela explains. "But I love what I do and I love these people. I love working with the elderly. They are so wise. We'd all be a lot better off if we listened to them more." My eyes scan the montage of thank-you notes from family members that are pinned up on Angela's bulletin board. People love Angela Shelton. "I love what I do. But when our children were little and my husband and I lived in Arizona, I did try to do something in the child abuse area." She sits down at her desk, and my eyes follow her. I have not heard this before. She never mentioned it during our phone calls. "I wanted to give something back to the community, so I volunteered down at the child abuse center. Wooweee . . ." She lets out a long breath demonstrating how hard that was. "I just couldn't do it. It just made me so sad. I mean I'd see these kids who had been left alone, abused, unfed. Their mothers would just leave them. It broke my heart. I couldn't do it. I was of no help to them because it made me so sad. So I know I can't work with kids. I can't do it."

"But you can work with the elderly."

"Yeah, but bless those who can work with the kids." She shakes her head as if remembering some awful story. I wonder if

I could handle doing what she does. I don't think I'd be able to see that much death. "But I learned a lot," Angela continues. "I learned that you bring your kids up to watch out for strangers, but nobody tells you to watch out for Uncle Joe—usually the familiar people are the abusers."

"My dad was the candy man."

"Exactly. They are usually right there in front of you. It is not the dark stranger. We need to educate people."

"We'd have to have one big message about denial, that's for sure. And reveal how manipulative the offenders are. And you know, not one of the perpetrators of any of the Angelas that I've met went to jail. Not one of them. And one of them was a cop. Nothing ever happened with my dad either. It seems like no one wants to believe that this stuff goes on, so people simply ignore it."

"But people do care. They just need to know. We need unity."

"That's what the New York Angela Shelton said." I notice Angela's computer screen for the first time. "Snap out of it" floats across her screen saver.

"I like your 'Snap out of it.'"

Angela laughs. "My friends think I'm harsh sometimes, but I really think you have to snap out of things. You can't let the whole he said, she said ruin you. And you can't let what someone else did to you ruin your life either." She looks right at me. I know full well what she means. I wonder what's going to make me snap out of it. "You can't let people ruin your life because of what they did. You have to put things aside. You have to forgive, but you can't ever forget. Because if you forget, the same thing might keep happening."

April 2002–almost a year after the search
Postproduction, Los Angeles

My editor's version of the movie was not accepted into the famous Sundance Film Festival. I tried submitting it to other festivals, and all of them rejected it. No studio, distribution company, TV network, or organization has offered to buy the movie either. I feel like I am in the fighting ring and I'm losing. I think about that dream I had where all the women were in the streets celebrating. I keep getting this feeling in my gut that the movie is not ready yet, that it needs to lead to that dream. I must be out of my mind. I told my editor about wanting to recut it, and he told me that he couldn't change anything without being paid more.

"You have to learn how to let it go," he said. "Some projects work out and some don't. You need to move on and do something else. You can't afford me anyway, honey bunny." He was right. I am out of money, my credit cards are almost maxed out again, and I don't want to keep borrowing more. So I sent him home and found a female editor whom I could afford. I'm really paying her on my credit cards, but she doesn't need to know that. I should have gone with a woman from the beginning since this is about inspiring women. I should just do it myself and quit trying to give it away, but I tell myself to shut up.

I sat in my little TV room crying and watched my first editor's version three times in a row. I made notes where it needed changes, and I handed them over to my new editor. I wonder what my therapist would say about all this. I bet she'd ask what's stopping me from cutting the movie myself. Handing this movie over to someone else is like having someone else go to therapy for me.

"A lot of this footage is just not going to cut together," my new editor warns. She's French and uptight, but I like her, and she's a lot cheaper than my first editor. I just nod, knowing that the footage is all there; she just needs to piece it together right.

"Just make sure it's really beautiful," I instruct her as the phone rings. It's an out-of-state number. I almost let it go to voice mail, but I decide to pick it up at the last minute. I immediately recognize the voice. It's my sister.

"Hey," I gasp excitedly, happy for the distraction from my film.

"Hey," she says quietly. She doesn't sound as excited as I am. "I just watched your movie. That was heavy."

"I'm redoing the whole thing," I tell her quickly, already annoyed that the older version is out in the world.

"Are you going to leave in the 'I forgive you' at the end?" Her words ring in my head. "I did not like that part." I had my first editor put the words "I forgive you" at the end of the movie before the credits roll. I feel like that is where I need to get to, and if the movie ends with that, then my art is ahead of me. It's kind of like my therapist saying that my intuition was ahead of me when I first began this movie.

"That forgiveness was more for myself than for him," I explain. "I feel like that's where I need to get to, so I put it at the end."

"I guess I can see that. I thought that was directed at him, and it made me sick. I mean I don't forgive Mom. I do have a relationship with her, but there are boundaries. I don't know—it's your dad. But my God, the hatred I have for that man."

"I know."

"I thought I'd dealt with a lot of it. But watching him, I mean . . . I realized that everything is not fine. I threw up all night."

"You did? I'm sorry."

"It's not your fault. It was just that at first, honestly, it felt like it was happening all over again. But I mean it's good that you did it and that you're getting it out there. People need to know that this is going on in perfectly 'normal' homes."

"The perfect American family."

"Exactly. But I don't have to forgive, and I probably never will."

"I'll send you the second version when it's done. It will be a lot different. I have a woman cutting it together now."

"It might take me awhile to watch it. I'm still messed up from the one I just finished. But I'm glad you're recutting it and I'm glad you're taking out the forgiveness. I hate that man." I get off the phone and go into my garage, which I have now transformed into an editing facility. My editor is cutting together a piece on my dad. I can see him over her shoulder. I wonder why I'm not angry. Why don't I hate him? I still love my dad. I feel like I'm in the middle of a seesaw and on one side is a realist who knows that my father is a freak and on the other side is the girl who remembers all the good times and wants her daddy back.

Dream Journal—June 20, 2001
    I dreamed I was trapped inside a small space and couldn't find my way out. "You have to get mad," someone said. "You have to release your rage in order to be released. You have to lose your mind in order to find it." I couldn't see anyone. The space was getting smaller and the walls were caving in. I was getting ready to scream.

Day 50 of the search
Somewhere in Georgia

I'm angry as I drive down the highway. I can't put my finger on where it's coming from. I just feel like I'm going to explode. My blood is boiling in my body. I can hardly concentrate on driving. This whole trip is hitting me suddenly, and I feel like I'm losing my mind. I cannot believe that I went to see my dad and just sat there and listened to him lie to my face. I think about Angela's screen saver with "snap out of it," but I want to beat the steering wheel and claw at my face instead. I don't know how to snap out of it. I'm so angry with myself for doing nothing. I want to drive the motor home into the concrete highway divider, but I have to get home to finish the movie. It has to inspire women. I have a mission, don't I? Maybe after I finish the movie, I can kill myself. I feel so stupid. Something is telling me to lose it. I quickly turn off on the first road I see and shut off the ignition. The crew looks at me, worried. I must have a very strange look on my face.

"Can you two go for a walk?" I motion for Chantal and Sylvia to leave the door. They both quickly stand up and head toward the exit. "Can you wire me?" I say to Giovanni, and I tell Gallo to get his camera. "I know it sounds weird, but I don't really care. I had a dream that I need to do this on camera. Otherwise, believe me, I'd go on a walk by myself. But I need to lose it. I'm so pissed off. You both just need to stay out of my way. But I need to show it in the movie. I had to stop this RV because I am so pissed off."

And then I lose it. I snap. My crew must think I'm nuts as they watch me scream like a banshee, but at this point there's nothing I can do about it. I can hardly keep myself from ripping the cabinets off the wall, but I need the security deposit back. I'm already going to lose some of the deposit from ripping the side of the RV off when I found out we were going to see my dad on Father's Day. "Dammit!" I throw my Angela Shelton binder across the floor. I want to claw my face, but I don't because of the camera. "I had to stop this RV because I am so pissed off. I can't believe that I sat there and talked to him the whole time and didn't yell at him." I'm so angry I don't know what to do. I turn around and grab hold of the foldout kitchen table and almost pull it off its hinges. "I had to stop and have a little therapy with my therapist. And I told her exactly what happened. He just sat there and denied everything. Everything!" I scream. Gallo and Gio back up into the other side of the RV. In some weird way I'm glad they are in here with me. I wish the camera wasn't on me though. I wish I could scratch my face. I feel like I am crazy, like everyone is going to think I'm crazy. But I have to talk about this. I have to reveal this pain. "My therapist says I should talk about this on camera too." Crap. What did she say earlier? I can't think straight. I wipe my face and compose myself as much as I can. "She talked about how it totally messes with my own reality. And you actually sit there and think that it really didn't happen. You start questioning yourself and your own reality when the abuser sits there and lies to your face." I run to my bag across the room and furiously fish inside it for the box of crayons I bought at a truck stop. I had them in my bag the whole time I was at my dad's. I got them so I could trigger his memory, but I never pulled them out. I never even brought them up. I didn't bring up so many things. I didn't even mention how my dad beat the hell out of all of us. I just sat there!

"I am so pissed off!" I yell and snap the crayons into pieces. I curse my dad over and over again and throw the crayons everywhere. I want to do more, but I am afraid of my own anger. I want space. I turn and explode out of the RV door. I storm off down the road. As I charge off down the dirt road, I notice that I've pulled off the highway alongside a graveyard. Even in my rage I see the irony and have to laugh out loud. The graveyard is my trigger back to reality. I take it as a reminder that I have to lay my father to rest. I have to snap out of it. I turn around and head back to the RV and start to cry. Why did I have to have this idea in the first place? I wish this movie was funny. I wish I was making a comedy.

2003—Two years after the search
Los Angeles

"Your dad is crazy, Ang!" Gallo yells into the phone. "My agent just called, and apparently I got some letter from your dad. He's suing me or something? Can he do that?" He sounds nervous. My mind goes blank.

"Are you kidding me?"

"No, Ang, I'm not kidding. And I'm a little freaked out. He can't sue me, can he?"

"No, give me a break. Why would he sue you anyway? I made the movie. And plus he signed a release." I'm confused. I sent my dad a copy of my second editor's version of the movie. I composed an email to him before I sent it. I wrote, "Dear Dad, it's another year and another Father's Day. I just thought I'd write to tell you I lead a great life that I love. If we can't face ourselves, we can face no one, and I just thought as my father, you'd like to know that I am facing myself and I hope you're doing the same." I wanted to put a "P.S. You're a prick," but I didn't. He responded saying that he hoped that *Searching for Angela Shelton* went well. So I sent him a copy of it and now he's threatening to sue me. I guess my father isn't really going to be my dream dad. I don't know why I even try to think otherwise.

I smoke five cigarettes in a row as I read the letter Gallo has faxed over to me. It is a cease and desist letter from an attorney who says he represents my father and my father's wife. The meat of it reads, "Mr. S was shown in the film without his consent and was repeatedly identified as a child-molesting and physically abusive father. Mr. S has always denied any such activity and if anyone had bothered to investigate Ms. Shelton's claims, they would have known that they were totally without substance." The letter goes on to say, "Both of my clients have been wrongly stigmatized by this film and each time it is shown, the damages grow. Mr. and Mrs. S advise that they were never presented releases. They are informed that Ms. Shelton has represented that she obtained a release from Mr. S; if so, that representation is false." And blah, blah, blah, it goes on and on and sounds like a whiny child who lost his toys in the sandbox.

I don't know what to do. I wonder if sending my father a copy of the movie was such a good idea. I feel stupid. Why do I always protect him? I thought I figured out that he is really not a good guy. It's like I forget, like my brain does not want to process that information. I don't know what it's going to take for me to see that my dad is not my savior and that he's a perpetrator. I think of my sister hating the word forgiveness at the end of the first version of my movie. I feel like I need to forgive myself for loving a perpetrator. I need to forgive myself for all the times I've hurt myself because of my inner pain. I feel like I'm running on a wheel again, repeating this lesson over and over again. I need a screen saver that says "snap out of it."

As if on cue, the phone rings and it is Angela Shelton Anonymous.

"My father just died," she states unemotionally. "I thought I'd call you." I stare straight ahead. This is just too weird to be weird anymore.

"Holy cow, you mean he just died? I'm so sorry, Angie."

"Yeah, I just left the hospital." I can hear her open and shut a door.

"Are you okay? How are you doing? You sound different."

"I'm sober," she says in huff like it's the most ridiculous thing imaginable. "I have been for a while. But not for long."

"Are you going to get drunk?"

"In just one moment."

"You don't have to. Please don't. Can you call your sponsor? Is there anyone there you can go see?"

She laughs and then begins to cry. "He's dead. He went, just like that. I tried to talk to him before but I figured, what's the point? He's an old man. What can he do about it? He doesn't even remember what he did."

"'Cause of the Alzheimer's?"

"He doesn't remember anything. So what does it matter?"

"He doesn't matter, to be honest. This is all about what you're doing to yourself because of what he did to you. He doesn't matter. It's about you. My dad is threatening to sue me if I don't stop this movie."

"Is he going to?"

"I have no idea. I think it's just a threat. He would have to go to court and prove that I am defaming him. We'd bring out all the old court documents. There are three children. He's just trying to get me to shut up, and so is his wife because they do not want to be found out. But you know what? They don't matter, just like your dad doesn't matter. What are we going to do now is the question. What are you going to do with your life? He's dead. How are you going to move on from him?"

"Get drunk."

"That's a choice."

"I couldn't confront him, Angela. I couldn't do it. I couldn't do what you did."

"It doesn't matter. The confrontation is more for you than for him. It's just like forgiveness. You have to forgive yourself. We have to forgive ourselves and love ourselves. We have to learn how to take care of ourselves." I feel like if I just keep talking to her that she will not fall down the slippery slope of repeated pain. "Everything we do affects everything else. It's your responsibility to change your own life though. You have a choice, Angela. Look at the other Angela Sheltons. Most of them were abused too, but an even higher number of them left the abusive husbands, put themselves through school, started their own businesses, got into therapy. You got sober . . ."

"For a minute."

"Yeah, well, it's all a process, right?"

"Right," Angela says. "I'm processing."

I look around my house that has turned into a postproduction facility. I am processing too. I have given my movie over to two people, hoping that they put me together, when in reality I'm going to have to cut this movie myself. I know it. It's just like I have to save myself. It's like a metaphor. I've just been avoiding it. And now I have no money, my own father has sent me a threat letter, and I'm faced with a choice. Just like Anonymous Angela. "You have the power to change your life, Angela. There are choices." I wonder what I'm going to do too. Do I keep giving my movie away and hoping someone else saves me? Or do I face my fear and learn how to work a machine? "What are you going to do now? Your dad is dead. He can't hurt you anymore, Angela. But you sure can hurt yourself."

"Oh God, I know. But what do I do now? What is the next step?" Angela asks like a little girl.

"You have to learn to love yourself. We both do." I can hear her open and shut a car door.

"They rolled out his body. They just rolled it out. He's gone."

We are silent. I don't know what to say. This is some heavy stuff. "Where are you right now?"

"At the liquor store."

Dream Journal—June 21, 2001
    I was riding the tricycle again in my dream last night, but this time I was coasting down the road alongside the RV. I no longer had to tug it. I was just floating beside it. I wasn't even pedaling

Day 51 of the search
Angela Shelton in Tennessee

We're headed west again toward California. We stop in Memphis to hopefully see an Angela Shelton who hasn't called me back. I decide not to be depressed about it. There are so many Angelas who have canceled, who have said I am crazy, who changed their minds, or who have just hung up on me, so I'm not upset if this one doesn't call back either. I think that I've met the Angela Sheltons I was meant to meet. There is one more left in New Mexico.

While we wait for the Angela in Memphis, we drive by the Lorraine Motel where Martin Luther King Jr. was shot. I pull up to the curb and park. We sit there in silence staring at the infamous motel room door on the second floor. I think about Dr. King's "I have a dream" speech and wish I had it committed to memory. I wonder if survivors will ever take to the streets and break the silence about sexual abuse and violence.

We wait for a while longer, but Angela Shelton never calls me back. So we go listen to the blues. We park right near all the blues bars and listen to live music all night. I am itching to dance. I think of the Missouri Angela Shelton driving for 80 miles to go dancing with her husband. I remember what she said about how I shouldn't care what people think and simply be myself. I have always been shy about dancing in public. I either have to be tipsy or at home alone with all of the lights turned off. If I look back at where the insecurity comes from, it probably started with my dad. It is probably tied to how he used to have my sister pose and be sexy for him and not me. Then I got into the pattern of being in relationships with people who told me to behave, to submit. I figure if I'm going to get better, I should begin immediately, so right there in Memphis I decide to give up my insecurity and dance like a loon right in front of everyone. We're in an empty blues bar with an awesome band, and the singer just happens to be blind. He can't judge me. He can't even see me. It's perfect. So I start dancing by myself. Sober. It's freeing and fun. I have no idea that I loved to dance so much or had so much pent-up energy. It's like a force in me waiting to be released. This is far better than ripping the sides of the walls off. I feel like I just grabbed a bit of my childhood back.

2004–Three years after the search
Postproduction, Los Angeles

I have decided to cut the movie myself. I don't know whether to claw my face or hug myself. I'm scared that this whole process is taking me too long. My second editor's version didn't sell, just like the first version. I made hundreds of copies of it and handed it off to publicists. I even had a manager and an assistant working on it. But it went nowhere. There was a part of me that was happy about that tragedy. Something keeps telling me that the movie's not selling is a blessing. It is almost as if the movie is playing a big joke on me; like it is its own entity and it will not do anything until I cut it myself. The early versions don't show the roller coaster of pain mixed with the inspiration, the faith, and the humor. I want to try to show all of that. I am ready to reveal myself, and I feel like if I don't do it now then I never will. When I announced to my team that I was going to read the manual and learn how to edit, they all told me I was crazy. They said that I was just having artistic butterflies and needed to move on to my comedy. They were all being paid on that project. They won't make any money if I follow my heart and finish this movie myself. There is a reason the other versions never went anywhere. I have to do this myself.

My editorial team freaked out. Some of them quit, and some of them got fired, but all of them told me I didn't know what I was doing and that I was crazy. It reminded me of families in denial who protect the perpetrator and ostracize the victim. It actually gave me the fuel to stand up for myself. And then nothing happened with my dad either. His threats stopped. My lawyer simply sent his lawyer a copy of the signed release along with the footage of what he said to me in his interview. That shut them up and I haven't heard a word since. Now I have no team, no father, and nothing else to focus on but this movie. I stare at the machine. Editing manuals surround me. I feel overwhelmed. I wish there was a manual on how to snap out of it. I feel like I'm staring at a vast ocean and I don't know how to swim. I know I have to just jump in. I have to do this myself. I feel so stupid that I didn't do this from the beginning. I want to rip the cord from the computer and smash it with a hammer. I smack myself across the face instead. I'm so stupid and this is taking me too long. I should have known this was going to happen. I should have kept my big mouth shut. I should have done a comedy from the beginning and never left on this trip. Smack.

Day 52 of the search
Angela Shelton driving . . .

There is nothing to do but drive. I drive and think, drive and think, think and drive. I'm trying to fit all this together in my head. Why did I have this idea in the first place? Why was there an Angela Shelton who was renting space to a foster care company? Why was the one who tracked sexual predators living in the same town as my dad? Does everything really happen for a reason? Why did so many of them cancel? Why were so many abused? Does that really make a comment on women in general? What am I supposed to do with this movie? What is my mission?

I feel like crying and screaming all at the same time. I don't have much farther to go, so I grip the wheel and stare straight ahead.

2003–Two and a half years after the search
Postproduction, Los Angeles

I can't stop crying. The episode of me on *Oprah* just aired. I met my hero. I went on national TV and told Oprah that she saved my life by telling her story. It was a dream come true. But I can't stop crying. I feel like I'm not ready for this, like I'm not cooked yet. I just started editing the movie myself—I'm not even done, and I'm receiving thousands of emails from people all over the world. I'm crying because of so many abuse stories that I'm hearing. I'm crying because the truth is that I really was searching for myself, and I found that not only was I not alone, but sexual abuse and violence is an epidemic like Lori said in the beginning. I'm crying because my computer makes a dinging sound when I receive an email and my office sounds like Vegas now. There are too many stories and it seems like others are all telling them to me. I'm getting flooded.

My therapist reminded me how I tend to take care of others before myself, and here I am taking care of other survivors. I'm cutting the movie all day and then I'm on the website all night answering emails from throughout the world. My therapist says I'm going to have to learn to take care of myself at some point. But I can't. It's as if I don't see myself as someone who needs to be, or deserves to be, taken care of. I'm seeing that there is an epidemic to address instead. There are too many stories. My inbox has 10,000 emails. People are grateful that I'm making this movie. Some of them even send me food. But I feel like I am failing and taking too long. I smack myself.

"I suggest you sit with these feelings and simply feel them," my therapist says. "Notice where the feelings come from and the memories they bring up. And then just sit with it and feel it. Feel it and heal it." I try it but I hate feeling. It reminds me of when I was little. I guess that's the point. When I was little and was being molested, I was not the first choice. My father preferred my sister. She was prettier. I was only molested when I was in the room with her, never when I was alone. I thought that I wasn't wanted, like I wasn't good enough. As I sit here feeling this, I realize that all the times I chose unavailable, angry men, I was trying to fix the relationship with my dad. I realize that I am so angry and have been stuffing it down, hiding it, covering it up with cigarettes, and laughing it off. That is sad and pathetic.

"You need to learn your own tools for self-care. You need to find a way to comfort yourself."

I hate therapy. I hate looking into the mirror. I sit and read thousands of emails instead. Out of the first 10,000 emails, there are only two stories where the offenders were caught, charged, and convicted. Both of the fathers started raping their daughters when the girls were 4 years old. Neither one of the men was sentenced to more than four years in jail. I am sick to my stomach. I read more stories and realize that there are so many people with the same story. The most consistent thing I read about is self-abuse. People share that they are overeaters, undereaters, alcoholics, drug addicts, and self-mutilators. I write back to many of them and tell them they should love themselves. "If there are so many of us doing the same thing, if we all got better and stopped self-abuse and healed, then we would create a dramatic shift in society," I write.

"Thank you," another email says. "Thank you for speaking for me because I cannot speak for myself." I wonder if they would still thank me if they knew I hated myself. I wonder what they would say if they knew I smacked myself across the face to relieve the stress. Maybe I should take my own advice and learn to love myself too.

"We want you to come speak at our support group. You are such a good teacher and an amazing voice," another survivor writes. I wonder what I would teach if I wasn't a hypocrite. I have an urge to hit myself, so I sit with it instead. I lay my hands on the desk in front of me and stare at them. I think about floating in the ocean. I give my hands over to the universe much like I gave my body over to the ocean. I just sit there. I think about the Angela in Virginia saying that one day it just started to get better. I don't hurt myself. It works. I wonder if that's like Anonymous Angela fighting the impulse for a beer. The desire to hurt myself fades. My email dings again.

"Thank you for doing this. You enabled me to come forward and tell my story. Thank you, Angela Shelton, for being as brave as you are." Tears flow down my face. These survivors emailing me have no idea that they are helping me just as much as I am helping them.

"Thank you," I write back.

Day 53 of the search
Somewhere in New Mexico

I remember my therapist saying this movie was going to lead to me having a catharsis. I haven't felt any catharsis yet. I wonder when it is coming. We have a couple of days left in New Mexico while we wait for our last Angela Shelton to meet with us. I sit and stare into space. I no longer feel alone. I feel like I am a part of something very big. I flip through my Angela Shelton binder.

2004–Three years after the search

I'm standing on the stage staring at about 300 people. They are standing up, applauding. I just received a standing ovation after I showed a rough version of my film. My silence is broken. It took me three years, but I put myself together. I cut the movie myself. I like it. I did a good job. I'm proud of myself. In three more months my movie will be available on the website. My name is now a dot-com. Colleges and universities are having me come to their campuses and speak. I've been to quite a few already. I not really sure what to say. I just tell them the story of how this all came to be. I am honest about my own story and I listen to the other stories. I have seen how this epidemic is not just a woman's issue. So many men have come up to me at these speaking engagements and told me about their abuse. I scan the audience, wondering which man will be the one to come up to me at the end of this speech. They all takes their seats again.

I love the faces in the crowd. I love that I decided to leave for my trip with no money and an idea. I love that it shook up my whole world and changed my life. It was worth it. "You want to know the real truth?" I ask the audience and they all laugh. I've been revealing lots of truths today. "Before I did this movie, I was sitting pretty. There was an awardwinning movie based on my life. I was making money. I modeled for years. I've been on the cover of magazines, gone out with male models, you name it. On paper I had accomplished a lot. But it wasn't until I was piecing myself together, literally, that I came face to face with the fact that I didn't even like myself. I went on a journey to survey women and discovered that I hated myself and I was full of rage. I could tell my therapist all about my dad and my abuse and my dating issues, but I never once told her that I was a self-mutilator." I look across the crowd staring at me. I see a few people nod and know already that they have the same issue. "I would beat myself up, scratch myself, smack myself, poke myself with pencils, you name it. I was full of rage. I was pissed. So you know how I have handled it? I have been in relationships with angry men because having to take care of their anger enabled me to not have to deal with my own. And the funny thing is that I've been single, and that's another joke on me because I made a movie about incest and a person doesn't get rich that way, and it's hard to get a date." Everyone laughs. "And for years I was taking all that pain and rage and turning it onto myself, and that is crazy. Now I can be a healthy crazy, not a crazy crazy." I grin and take a deep breath and ask if there is anyone who would like to share his or her story.

A woman raises her hand and I call on her. She stands up and starts taking off her jacket. I laugh, thinking she is really getting ready for a fight. She moves up to the stage. "Thank you," she says nervously. "Thank you for what you are doing. You are doing it for all of us. I'm so afraid to tell my story."

"Tell it then." I take off my microphone and hand it to her. She looks at me in shock. I look at the audience for some encouragement and they nod to her too.

"You're an angel, you really are," she says as she takes the microphone from me. "I have been to the survivor groups. I've been to therapy, but even with all the work I have done, I still beat myself up." She looks at me and we nod to each other. We can see each other and see what we are both doing. It is like looking in the mirror. "I continue to abuse myself in a bunch of ways. It started when I was very young. I'm trying to find my purpose in life. I try to be a normal person, but inside I still don't believe that I'm good enough to do anything, you know?"

"Yeah, I do know."

"I do believe that everything happens for a reason. I can't believe I'm standing up here with Angela Shelton." I want to tell her that I do not claim that name as my own, that my name and my movie helps me as much as it helps her. I just smile at her instead. She smiles back at me nervously and then continues. "I was molested, I was abused, oh, and I was raped when I was 16 too. But I'm learning to love myself again. This is powerful stuff that you're doing, Angela. You're right. If we all talk about it, if we all share it and are not ashamed or embarrassed or fearful . . . So many times we don't want to believe our own stories because we want our moms or our dads or our stepdads or whoever did it to love us."

"That is so right. That's it. We all want to be loved," I tell her and want to pull her to me and hold her.

"I know it, and I'm just learning to love myself," she says. "Anyway, I'm glad I met you. I'm sorry I'm rambling."

"Don't apologize." She hands me the microphone and starts to get down off the stage. "Hey." I stop her and she turns to me. "I promise that I will never hit myself again if you promise not to hurt yourself either."

She stares at me. "Oh God. Really?" She looks at the floor and then takes a step toward me. I think about all the emails I've received. I think about Anonymous Angela. I think about how many beautiful people are hurting themselves because of what someone else did to them. I feel like if we all stopped the self-abuse and self-hatred, then it would make a difference. The woman stares at me and then says, "OK. I promise that I won't hit myself, hurt myself, or abuse myself or use all the other tricks I have to harm myself. I'm looking you in the eyes and I promise I will not do it anymore." We shake hands.

"Me either. I promise." We hug and the audience stands up and applauds.

That is the hardest commitment I have ever made, but I keep my promise.

Dream Journal—June 24, 2001
I dreamed that a scab came off my body that had been there for years. I woke up feeling irritated that it had been there for so long I hadn't noticed it. Removing it was disgusting. The dream was so vivid I can almost get a hint of the smell of old blood. It hurt and I was pissed. But as I woke up I was relieved that it was gone.

Day 54 of the search
Angela Shelton in New Mexico

It seems like we've been on the road for years. My crew and I finally passed Texas. That was a feat in itself. There were a few Angela Sheltons there, but we didn't stop for them. I don't have the gas money, and they still were not sure they wanted to talk, so we kept heading west. The sky is so ridiculously beautiful in New Mexico that it feels like we're driving into heaven. The rain lifted after I saw my dad and it hasn't sprinkled since. We have made it to the land of enchantment.

We are getting closer to the end of this trip. I don't know how I'm going to continue, let alone put this story together. I've sold every stock I ever owned. I haven't been able to take jobs back in Los Angeles because I'm out in the middle of nowhere searching for myself. My agent is irritated with me. I've depleted all my savings accounts and mutual funds. I have no other money coming in. I'm starting to get nervous as the days are marked off the calendar. I had no idea that making a movie was so expensive. I get the feeling that I should just trust and know that I'm protected and this will all work out. I think about the Angela Sheltons and how most of the ones I talked to talked about God. Maybe I should take a page from the Angela Shelton journal.

Dream Journal—June 24, 2001

I dreamed that I was sold into slavery. I was in an underground slave trade run by rich white men. They looked like androids, perfectly ironed and starched, perfectly put together. They all had on fake smiles that gave me the creeps. I had found the secret corridors that led outside. I could see the captors on the other side of the wall. They were trading people and little children. I had found a way out of a maze of dark rooms and was secretly saving them. The password was my name. Groups of men and women and children were whispering "Angela Shelton" as they moved through underground corridors. More and more people were coming forward. We were escaping. I was at the head, leading them out into the light. I could see the white android-looking men coming after us,

but the wall blocked them I had found
the secret passage and the secret password,
and it was my name. I could hear people
whispering "Angela Shelton, Angela Shelton,
Angela Shelton," and the sound of little feet
running for safety.

2004—Three years after the search
Somewhere in America

"I know who the anonymous Angela Shelton is." I turn to
the survivor I'm talking to. No one knows who Anonymous
Angela is except my crew.

"What're you talking about? No, you don't," I say.

"Yes, I do. You didn't hide it that well—the map. You had a
star on her town on the map. You held it up in the movie."

"What did you do, pause the movie and zoom in? There were
lots of stars on towns we never made it to. There were quite a
few Angelas that canceled."

Then she tells me the name of Anonymous Angela's town
and the street she lives on. "I knew it the moment I started
watching your movie. I knew from the very first moment. I
recognized her voice. I knew who she was. I've even gotten
drunk with her."

"Wow, you do know her. That's so random and weird. How do
you know Anonymous Angela? You don't even live in that town."

"I used to. We used to share a fence post. She was my
neighbor."

I freeze. I feel like I just got socked in the stomach. I stare
at this lady. She told me her story yesterday. She told me about

how she was raped at the age of 3 and then her grandfather started prostituting her out from his basement when she was 5. Men gave money to her grandfather and then raped her violently and often. I stare at her. She stares back. I think of Anonymous Angela. All the pieces from both of their stories flood my brain. That town. I remember how small it was. They were neighbors. The abuse was happening right next door to each other. That means that Anonymous Angela's dad could have been one of the abusers of this lady. I'm confused, sickened, and sad.

"And my grandfather just passed away," this woman tells me. "I'm inheriting that house."

"You are? Wow. What are you going to do with it?"

"Burn it to the ground."

"Are you really? Can I film it?" I throw in before she has a chance to answer.

"No," she says quickly. "I'm not ready to come out with my story like you. I'll just live vicariously through you like thousands of others. Thank you." We're nearing the airport where she's dropping me off. She insisted on giving me a ride. I just spoke at her college. She insisted on some alone time with me. I thought she was planning on telling me more of her story. I was not expecting the Anonymous Angela connection. Angela Sheltons are everywhere. "I don't take it lightly when someone changes my life," she says. "People need to meet you, they need to hear you, and I'm going to help that to happen." She looks over at me and giggles at my blank stare. I remember last night when she told me her story. I was the one who threw up. She held my hair as I cried and puked into the toilet after hearing the horrors of her life and how an entire family and most of the town hid the abuse. I've heard thousands of stories at this point. I have cried and hugged many survivors, but this woman's story and her connection to the Anonymous Angela Shelton has hit me harder than any of them.

"I was meant to see you on TV. And I was meant to order that DVD from your website. And I was meant to meet you. You changed my life and it's that simple." She pulls to the curb. I clutch my bag.

"I can't believe you were neighbors with Anonymous Angela. It's just too weird."

"It's not weird, Angela. It's God."

She drives off waving and seems so happy. My eyes well up so much that it takes me a moment to find my airline. I usually fall asleep immediately on airplanes, but I stare straight ahead for most of this trip. The connections that keep appearing are too weird to be weird anymore. When I land in Los Angeles I turn on my cell phone that also gets my email. I watch the little lightning bolt shoot all my new messages into my in-box. I am shocked when I see Angela Shelton's name appear. It's Anonymous Angela. I haven't heard from her in months. All the hairs stand up on my arms, and my eyes well up again when I open it. I stumble down the aisle, pulling my roller bag and slinging my backpack over my shoulder while reading her email.

"I just want to let you know that I'm doing really well," she writes. "I went into recovery again and I'm still sober. It's been 145 days. I just thought I'd check in with you and say hi. It seems like so many good things are happening. I feel like there are a lot of angels around. And I just wanted to say thank you for being in my life, for calling me that one time. I love you."

"I love you too, Angela Shelton," I write back. "You have no idea how many angels are around you right now."

Dream Journal—June 25, 2001

I dreamed I was in the desert I had been walking for what seemed to be an eternity. I look at my bare feet. They are bloody and swollen. I can't move them at all. I came out of the dream so slowly. I sat up and rubbed my feet. They were aching like I had just walked for miles.

Day 55 of the search
Angela Shelton in New Mexico

"You're my last Angela, and I'm really sad."

"Well, no, you're the last one," the Angela Shelton in New Mexico points out. She's half Caucasian and half African-American. She's also a Muslim who was raised as a Catholic. "My Muslim name is Malakai, which means "angel" in Arabic, and it's both the man's name and the woman's name." I love that it includes men and women. I think about my brother and everything he went through.

She converted when she met her husband. She works at the hospital in the newborn nursery ward just like the Angela Shelton in Virginia. Angela Shelton has eight kids of her own. Her husband is an artist and stays at home while she works. I can relate to that. I've supported men more than once in my life.

"What do you think about what I'm doing? What did you think about when I first called you?"

"I thought, man, this girl is conceited. I wish I had an ego that big." She shrugs her shoulders up in an apologetic girlish way.

I am speechless. "Really? Do I give that impression?" She shrugs again. "But this isn't about me," I point out. Angela isn't buying it. I am an egomaniacal, conceited Hollywood weirdo in her eyes. It depresses me for a moment. Self-hatred creeps into my mind, and I wonder why I decided to make this movie in the first place. I tell myself to snap out of it. I'm meeting the last Angela Shelton. I need to pay attention.

Angela has to get back to work, so I've made a time to meet her at her house. On the drive there I ask my crew if they think I'm an egomaniac, and the fact that they don't answer quickly makes me feel like a jerk.

"You're driven," Gallo says.

"You have a vision," Chantal adds. I figure that they hate me. If I'm going to be thought of as an egomaniac by everyone, I figure there are worse things. The movie is called *Searching for Angela Shelton,* for crying out loud.

Angela Shelton's husband never comes into the living room while we are in her house. I wonder if he thinks I'm full of myself too. The crew and I sit and talk with Angela on the sofa with seven of her eight kids instead. "So, Angela, explain to me your headdress." I stare at the scarf she has tied around her head. I've seen Muslim women wear them on TV, but I have no idea what the symbolism is.

"It says in the Koran to wear it so you'll be recognized as a Muslim and not be molested," Angela explains, and then she giggles. I'm confused. Does that mean it's okay to molest women without headdresses? I've always heard that Muslim women were pretty abused by their men, but I don't push the subject. I don't want to cause any trouble, and I get the feeling we should really get out of here as quickly as we can. It feels like they don't really want my crew and me here. It's strange. I try to act nice and smile and pay attention to the children. They have no judgment. "I don't wear it at the hospital," Angela explains, touching her headdress. "I'm an information gatherer, and it's about the patient and not about me. I don't want to put someone into a position where they'll start asking me questions when the visit is about them." All I want to do is ask her questions, so I guess she has a point. "Are you disappointed with your Angela Sheltons?" she asks after a moment.

"God, no. They're very inspiring. I love all of them." I even love her. I'm sad to leave her because this is the last one, but I follow my intuition and get the crew packed up. We need to let Angela and her family have their evening together. I'm done. There is not another Angela between here and home.

While walking away from her house and back to the RV, I don't feel the ground again. I am officially finished with my search for Angela Sheltons and I can't feel my feet.

2004—Three years after the search
Los Angeles

I get an email with "Rosie O'Donnell" as the subject line. The email says, "You are speaking for all of us." It is signed by Rosie. I'm sitting in an airport when it comes in. I laugh and reply with my phone number, calling the person's bluff. When my phone rings and it is actually Rosie O'Donnell on the other end, I almost slide off my seat in shock. "What do you need?" she asks. I sit there staring at the other people, waiting for my flight home. Some of them stare back. I must have laughed too loud. I'm not sure how to answer Rosie's question. I'm in Washington, D.C. They just showed a big portion of the movie on TV on *48 Hours Investigates*. I spoke in front of a Congressional hearing. I told them about all the survivors who are contacting me and how sexual and domestic violence is an epidemic. I'm not sure what I need though, besides money to eat and finish this movie. "You're doing this for all of us. I'm an Angela Shelton too," Rosie says. "What do you need in order to finish this movie?"

"To not be kicked out of my house in the process of making it would be great," I tell her, thinking of my house being on the market. I've gone through all of my other savings. Selling my house to keep the movie going is my last option.

"I'm going to help you, but you have to promise that you will take care of yourself in this process. Please don't let this work drain you," Rosie urges. I cannot believe that Rosie O'Donnell is telling me this. I'm not sure what to do. I promise her that I will take care of myself. "Good. Send me your address. I'll send you some money."

Rosie kept her word and sent me the money I needed to pay my mortgage for the last few months it took me to finish the movie. Rosie saved my house. I took it off the market. I rush to my therapist's office to tell her. She grins at me.

"I had a dream about you," my therapist tells me. I have a flash of the tricycle from one of my recurring dreams. I look past her to the huge dream catcher she has hanging on her wall. It's missing something. I look closer and see that the net is not there. I've never noticed that before. I wonder how a dream catcher can catch dreams without a net, but I don't bring it up. "I dreamed that you jumped out of a plane, but you were wearing a parachute and you were glowing with so much love and hope that it lit up everything in the sky. It was very colorful, very beautiful." She smiles as she looks me in the eyes. "I don't know why I'm telling you my dream in your session. I just thought you'd like to know that. It was such a beautiful image."

"That's really cool. And fitting. I am jumping in a way. I'm coming out into the world and breaking my silence and showing people how I got better."

"And that, in turn, will help them get better."

"I hope so. But it does feel like a leap I'm taking, like falling from the sky with a parachute."

"It will all work out," my therapist promises. She's smiling. I smile back. "It's really not good protocol to tell you this," she says as we both stand up, ending my 50-minute session. "But because of all that you're doing, I just thought you'd like to know that I'm a survivor too." I am floored. "You really are speaking for all of us, Angela. And you're doing a good job. Don't give up." I promise not to. "And take care of yourself during the process." I nod, remembering Rosie telling me the same thing. I leave the office thinking about my own therapist being a survivor. It is amazing how making this movie has opened my eyes.

I get home and have an email waiting for me with the subject line "I was your dad's neighbor." My mouth drops open in shock as I read. "I lived next door to your dad and his wife for about 15 years. Before your movie your dad was a close family friend. He came to my graduation from high school. I went to his wedding. While I was living next door to your dad, my stepfather was abusing me. I literally went into shock when I just happened to be watching your movie and it was your dad who opened the door. Since that moment I have been slowly dealing with my own abuse. Seeing you and your dad on TV was a really big event in my life. I'd just like to share the unique effect your movie had on me. You made a great movie. I've shared it with lots of people. Take care." I feel like everything is poring in at once or like I just jumped out of an airplane.

I go to the bathroom and throw up. I can see the vans on my dad's street in my mind. I can see every street I ever lived on. I think about how many thousands of emails I've been receiving since I first started searching for Angela Sheltons. This survey of women goes far beyond me and my namesakes. I don't know what to do about it. I wish I could help everyone. It's like I told my brother: I feel like I'm on a crusade to fix all the things that my dad ever did to kids. But what about all his neighbors? I vomit again and think about Rosie and my therapist and wonder how I'm supposed to take care of myself.

Day 56 of the search
Somewhere in Arizona

It's our last night together. This journey wasn't just about Angela Shelton. I had four crewmembers in the RV with me the whole time. I splurge on a semifancy meal to celebrate our last night together. My crew has not only been stuck together for two months, but all of them have been with me for one of the most crucial times in my life. Each one of them shares his or her stories and listens to everyone else's. It is like a graduation ceremony before we all head home. In honor of their privacy, I won't reveal their pasts, but I will say this: Only one of my crewmembers wasn't abused as a child. Four out of five of them lived through physical abuse, sexual abuse, or rape. Our last meal together is emotional. We share a group hug.

The one who has not lived through violence is stunned. None of us knows what to do. This trip has had an effect on us that will be with us forever.

I'm just settling in bed to process this whole trip when Gallo comes rushing into the RV. I sit up, worried that a catastrophe has fallen upon us on our last night. "That documentary is on HBO," he announces. "That one about the guy who had all the other guys with his name over for dinner."

"Alan Berliner? That was fast."

"Yeah, it's on TV right now. Come up and watch it." The girls and I follow him to the hotel room he is sharing with Giovanni. I can't believe HBO put that movie together so fast. I wonder if I'll be able to do mine that quickly. We all gather around the tiny TV in Gallo's room and watch the movie that I was told was the reason HBO didn't fund mine.

"I cannot believe this is on TV on our last day of filming," Chantal says.

Alan Berliner's movie is about his name. He dissects it, searches through the history of it, and talks about his name for the whole movie. Then he invites 12 of his namesakes over for dinner. I wonder how many of them have seen violence. My movie isn't about not naming your child Angela Shelton or that every Angela Shelton is a victim of abuse. It's about something bigger than a name.

"Well, look on the bright side," I say. "This means no one owns the movie. It's survivor owned and survivor run, not studio owned or studio run."

"Everything happens for a reason," Chantal says.

2004–three years after the search
Somewhere

My brother flies out to Los Angeles for a visit. He's staying at my house with his boyfriend. It's the first time he's been here. We're both beside ourselves and stay up talking all night, chattering like schoolgirls. I have so many questions to bombard him with. It's like I haven't had a brother, or a dad, in my life. I feel like I'm a volcano of need.

"I hate to bring up our childhood again, and I don't want it to be the subject every time we get together." My brother nods at me like he doesn't want it to be the subject du jour either. "But I have a question for you. I have this issue that I noticed, and now that I've been propelled into the world of getting better and being a speaker and a teacher, I feel like I have to address everything, you know?" He nods, waiting. I swallow hard. "Did anything weird ever happen in the bathroom? I have this thing about not being able to close the bathroom door. Even when I'm in someone else's house, I tend to leave it wide open, or at least a crack, while I'm in there. It's strange, but I feel more comfortable that way. It's like a part of me does not want to close the bathroom door. Isn't that weird? So since you're here and you did share in my abusive past, I was just curious if you remember anything about the bathroom. I might as well confront every last issue while you're here, right?" I joke. Steve stares at me. He's white.

"Honey, you don't remember that?"

I suddenly feel ill. "Remember what?" My mind is racing. I'm shuffling through catalogs, looking through boxes in the attic of my mind, but I find nothing. Steve looks at me tenderly like I'm a little girl again. I think about the photo album of Polaroids that my dad kept that I could not for the life of me recall.

"Honey, your dad used to take you into the bathroom and shut the door."

I have to throw up. I go into the bathroom and vomit. I stare at the toilet bowl and look across the room at the wide-open door. I think about the girl who sent me an email when she saw me on TV. She had been about to kill herself. She had the razor ready and her plan plotted out. She couldn't take it anymore. She had been sexually abused and she hated herself because of it, so she was going to take her life to get away from the pain.

"I was going to do it. But my TV was on, and I heard you talking, and you spoke about how you hated yourself too. That's when I dropped the razor out of my hand," this young girl wrote. "You made me not kill myself. Thank you, Angela Shelton, for speaking out. I heard you. Thank you for giving me my life back."

I stare at the toilet bowl and think about that girl. I have no idea where she lives or what her full story is. I'm just glad she didn't kill herself. I lean over and kick the bathroom door closed and sit there on the floor, alone in the bathroom. I bet that girl would want me to take my bathroom back. I bet she'd be glad that I shut my door. I get up and flush, brush my teeth, and open the door. My brother is standing there, looking very worried.

"It's OK," I assure him. "I'm OK. But you know what? I don't want to know the details. I don't want to have to go charge through my past and find out more horrible things that my dad did. I've already been dealing with enough. I don't want to add more to the pile. I was just sitting there thinking, what can I do now? How can I move forward and take control back right now? I can shut the damn door."

My brother hugs me. "That's a good choice."

Day 57 of the search
The last day of the search, Los Angeles

We drive full-speed ahead. We arrive back into Los Angeles in the afternoon light. We have completed a very large wobbly circle around the United States. I look down at the speedometer and see that we drove more than 13,000 miles.

"I can't believe we actually did this," Chantal says for all of us.

"Now comes the hard part," Gio points out. "You have to put all this together. We get to go home, but you're left with the movie."

We all hug like we're leaving summer camp. I drop each one of my crewmembers off in the same order as I picked them up two months ago. I drive the RV back up my hill alone. I feel different. I'm not sure what to do now. I think about all the Angelas as I unload the boxes of tapes. My survey of women in America showed me that we are all pretty amazing and we've been through hell, but most of us are breaking the cycle and leading awesome lives. I hope to follow in their footsteps. I thought I was going to make a movie that inspired women, and here I am the most inspired. I feel blessed to have met these Angela Sheltons. I feel honored to share their name. I hope this movie helps somebody like it helped me. I think about Anonymous Angela and hope she's doing well. I think about Lori at the gas station and feel my head to make sure her peace-of-heart pin is still in my hair. It is.

Yesterday

"I'm still sober," Anonymous Angela writes. "I thought I'd write to you. I'm a year sober now. I think about you all the time. I will never forget meeting you. Hope all is going great with you. If you get a chance, let me know how you're doing."

"Wow. Good for you, Anonymous! I'm so proud of you. I think about you all the time too!"

"I love your movie, by the way. It took me awhile, but I finally watched it. I knew it was going to bring up a lot, though, so I waited. I wanted to make sure it didn't send me back there. But it was inspiring. I loved it. And it was funny in places too. Really funny."

"I told you I wanted to make a comedy. Are you happy being sober?"

"Yes, I am. I still have my bad days, but I handle them a lot better by not drinking. It's a much different place to just be myself and not rely on a drink to be able to speak." I don't tell her about her old neighbor that I met. I don't say anything about her town or her abuse; I don't want to bring it up. I want to focus on the positive, on the healing.

"I quit self-abuse," I write back. "All this time of knowing you, I never told you that I beat myself up. Talking to you was a huge part of what opened my eyes. We have the same issues; we just have different tools. I chain-smoked cigarettes and beat myself up. I used to smack myself, pinch myself, you name it. I never even realized where it came from until after I made this movie. But I quit. I had to. I quit smoking too."

"That's so great. I had a great counselor during treatment. She helped me a lot with the issues with my dad. I finally feel at peace. I'm sorry I covered up that pain with addictions."

"When we stay in those dark places, we just help the abuse continue. I'm glad you talked about your dad. I've let go of my rage as well. I dance to Led Zeppelin instead of abusing myself now. And all that time I spent barking at you to love yourself made me learn to do the same. This work really made me love people. I love you! It dawned on me that if I love other people so much, then I have to love myself too. And if I love myself, I can't harm myself. It's kind of rude. It's like harming you if I harm myself, and I want you to be safe from harm. I don't want you to hurt yourself because of what some jerk did to you. I don't care if it was your father. So I have to practice what I preach, so I quit. It's been years since I last hurt myself."

"I'm sorry that you did that. You never told me that. I'm glad you're speaking about it now and being so open and honest. You're an awesome woman. I go to your website a lot. You're doing wonderful things. Keep up the good work. You're speaking for a lot of people." I have a flashback to the dream I had where people were whispering our name as a password to escape.

"Thank you! I had no idea I would end up being an expert in trauma. I have received thousands of emails from all over the world, and the similarities of all the stories are amazing. There are millions of us. But if every survivor healed and stopped self-abuse, then we really could change the world just by changing our own lives. Then the victims don't turn into perpetrators or get into relationships with them. We could break the cycle. Like healing yourself heals the world. Healing is an act of revolution."

"I'm one of those who is healing. I'm sorry it took me this long to get better. But I do feel a lot happier. Life is getting much better. I'm sorry you were on my drunk dial list."

"No need to apologize. It's never too late. Look what's happening! Life works in mysterious ways, doesn't it? Who knew that *Searching for Angela Shelton* would end up changing people's lives? But it changed mine."

"It changed mine too. I'm glad I called you back. I'm glad you went searching for us."

"Me too." I smile at her even though she can't see me. "I love what I found."

FINDING ANGELA SHELTON

Resources

Thank you for reading this book. I hope that it sparked some thoughts as well as some conversations. If you or someone you love is being abused right now or if you are in crisis, contact 800/656-HOPE or visit rainn.org, which has an online hotline as well.

If you are a concerned citizen, loved one of a survivor, or an offender or potential offender, there are great resources at Stop It Now! (stopitnow.org).

To prevent abuse in your community—train the adults on how to recognize and react responsibly. The national statistics say that one in four girls and one in six boys will be sexually abused in their lifetime. A great way to prevent abuse is to minimize opportunity for it to happen! A training that I approve of and have taken myself is the Stewards of Children Training from Darkness to Light. Visit darknesstolight.org. The training also provides information about what to do if you know of children being abused.

If your child or a child you know of is involved in the court system, is a victim of abuse, and has a case number, contact BACA—Bikers Against Child Abuse (bacausa.com). BACA is a shield against further abuse. BACA also goes to court with the children. I myself am a BACA child and BACA protects me too. I love BACA!

If you are a survivor at any point on your pathway to healing, visit The Survivor Manual at survivormanual.com. I have enlisted a collection of experts to answer the myriad questions that come with surviving. You'll find a list of healing techniques, resources, videos, and more. Thank you for healing—by healing yourself, you heal the world!

"Bad things may have happened to you, but it's your decision how the rest of the story goes."
—Angela's brother, Steve

BOOK CLUBS

You, your book club, or organization could get a 30-minute call with Angela. Visit findingangelashelton.com to be a part of the movement and the *Finding Angela Shelton* Challenge. We can create dramatic social change by starting conversations.

Thoughts to ponder while discussing the book in your class, group, club, or meeting:

Go around the room and share your personal experiences with trauma.

How many people who have experienced trauma do you know?

Have you ever experienced any kind of trauma? Were you silent about it and if so, why? Now is a great opportunity to break your silence.

When experts estimate that one in four girls and one in six boys will be sexually abused before their 18th birthday, why are Angela's statistics so different?

How does abuse affect our society?

How does one person's healing affect the whole world?

What are some ways to break the cycle of abuse?

How early should you talk to your kids about abuse and how would you approach it?

If you were in Angela's situation, would you have confronted your father? What would you have done differently?

After reading this book, how have your thoughts about violence been confirmed or changed?

How can you as a group or an individual break the silence and cycle of abuse?

How can one voice change the world? How are you going to do it?

ACKNOWLEDGMENTS

I wish to thank everyone who encouraged me, helped me, listened to me, loved me, fed me, and protected me while I processed and then released my story into the world.

Katherine Cortez, Lanette Phillips, Tracy Mazuer, John Waszak, Aly Drummond, Wendy Murphy, Anne Lee, Matthew Kelly, Tammie Johnson, Heidi Schanz, Kerry Rossow, Ophelia-Dawn Shona Power, Brent King, Eric Feig, Eric Leemon, David Matthiessen, Jim Hardy, Zak Kilberg, Shawn-Caulin Young, and Steven Cox. A special thanks goes to Kat Blodget, Shendl Diamond, and Tudor Boloni, who read my very first draft and told me to keep going.

Hooray for Kari Greenfield, my editor Alrica Goldstein, and everyone at Meredith Publishing. I never expected the experience with a publishing house to be so dreamy. I am very grateful to Kathleen Anderson for being the first professional who gave me the thumbs-up in the book world and to Marlene Adelstein for excellent notes.

I am especially grateful to Kimberly Zarley and Pam Kvitne, who saw me speak at the Lutheran Church of Hope in Iowa and made it a personal campaign to get my book published.

A big fat squeeze to my family: Joann Shelton, Helen Shelton, Susie and Toby Shelton, my cousins Jodi and Jeremy, and to my brother and sister Steve and Lisa whom I claim as kin and refuse the "step."

I could never have reached this point in my life without the support of everyone who invested in Searching for Angela Shelton *and continues to believe in the movie that turned into a movement: Mark Ordesky, Jamie Kennedy, Chantal Moore, Marcus Allen, George Penny, Marietta Boloni, Natasha Boloni, Karen Catchpole, Eric Mohl, Scott Salter, Carol Micheluz, Anna Micheluzzi, Katherine Scott, and Eric Gold. And thank you to my crew who went on the road with me and survived over 13,000 miles across America: Chantal Moore, Christopher Gallo, Giovanni Di Simone, and Sylvia Johnson. A special thanks goes to Rosie O'Donnell for shocking me by paying my mortgage for three months while I finished editing the documentary.*

A humongous thank you goes to Angela Sheltons everywhere. Thank you for returning my calls and emails and trusting that I was not a telemarketer. Also a big thanks to the Angelas who thought I was crazy and never believed me. You inspired me just as much. A delicate thanks goes to the Angelas who remained silent. I understand.

And last, but in no way least, Abraham Ingersoll, who assured me that I could edit the movie myself and supported me while I did it and who told me that I needed to write this book and barked at me incessantly until I began the process. This journey would never have been the same without you. Thank you.